eForth

as Arduino Sketch

no extra Programmer

Chen-Hanson Ting

The current Forth Bookshelf can be found at
https://www.amazon.co.uk/Juergen-Pintaske/e/B00N8HVEZM

1 Charles Moore - Forth - The Early Years: Background information about the beginnings of this Computer Language
2 Charles Moore - Programming A Problem Oriented Language: Forth - how the internals work
3 Leo Brodie - Starting Forth -The Classic
4 Leo Wong – Juergen Pintaske – Stephen Pelc FORTH LITE TUTORIAL: Code tested with free MPE VFX Forth, SwiftForth and Gforth
5 Juergen Pintaske – A START WITH FORTH - Bits to Bites Collection – 12 Words to start, then 35 Words, Javascript Forth on the Web, more
6 Stephen Pelc - Programming Forth: Version July 2016
7 Brad Rodriguez - Moving Forth / TTL CPU / B.Y.O. Assembler
8 Tim Hentlass - Real Time Forth

9 Chen-Hanson Ting - Footsteps In An Empty Valley issue 3
10 Chen-Hanson Ting - Zen and the Forth Language: EFORTH for the MSP430G2552 from Texas Instruments
11 Chen-Hanson Ting - eForth and Zen - 3rd Edition 2017: with 32-bit 86eForth v5.2 for Visual Studio 2015
12 Chen-Hanson Ting - eForth Overview
13 Chen-Hanson Ting - FIG-Forth Manual Document /Test in 1802 IP
14 Chen-Hanson Ting - EP32 RISC Processor IP: Description and Implementation into FPGA – ASIC tested by NASA
15 Chen-Hanson Ting – Irriducible Complexity
16 Chen-Hanson Ting - Arduino controlled by eForth
17 Chen-Hanson Ting – eForth as Arduino Sketch – no Programmer needed

18 Burkhard Kainka - Learning Programming with MyCo: Learning Programming easily - independent of a PC (Forth code to follow soon)
19 Burkhard Kainka - BBC Micro:bit: Tests Tricks Secrets Code, Additional MicroBit information when running the Mecrisp Package
20 Burkhard Kainka – Thomas Baum – Web Programming ATYTINY13
21 Georg Heinrichs - The ATTINY Project – Why Forth?
22 Dr. Karl Meinzer - IPS – a Forth-like Language for Space

All available as eBook – many of them as Print Book as well.

Contents

Part One: eForth_328 for Arduino Uno

Part Two Metacompilation of ceForth_328

File: ceForth_328.pdf converted A5 v12 Print Book

Link to additional information:

https://wiki.forth-ev.de/doku.php/projects:430eforth:start#arduino_uno_und_arduino_nano

more to be added probably based on feedback

eForth as an Arduino Sketch

Last year I decided to retire from electronics and microcontrollers, because after two glaucoma and cataract operations, I could not see small objects and narrow lines and there was no way that I could work on surface mounted parts with very narrow line spacing. So I cleaned out my study and my garage, gave away all my tools and spare parts. I realized that I should not be a hardware engineer. I am only a programmer, and should just work on software.

Then, when I visited my brother in Denver last summer, I saw that my niece was working on a couple of Arduino Boards. On an Arduino board, there was a microcontroller in a DIP socket! That was very interesting. When I came back, I bought a couple of Arduino Uno Boards, and have been working on them since. I had to buy back tools and many electronic parts and ate my vow to stay away from hardware.

Arduino Uno is a lovely, small, cheap, and readily accessible microcontroller board. The operating system and the programming environment Arduino 0022 is a good match to the Arduino Uno Board. Through a single USB cable, you can upload programs from a PC to Arduino Uno, and then communicate with the Uno through the same cable using RS232 protocol. You write programs in C language as sketches in Arduino 0022, and the sketches are compiled and then uploaded to the ATmega328P microcontroller on Arduino Uno for execution. Sketches are C programs greatly simplified to the point that you just have to fill lines of code in the two following routines:

```
setup()
```

```
loop()
```

All intricacies and complications in the C language and its associated compiler and linker are taken care of by the Arduino 0022 system. No wonder Arduino is such a huge success.

FORTH is a programming language much better suited for microcontrollers than C. FORTH is really a programming language with a built-in operating system. It has an interpreter and a compiler so that you can write programs in small modules and interactively test and debug them. You can build large applications quickly and debug them thoroughly. FORTH also gives you access to all the hardware components in the microcontroller and all of the IO devices connected to the microcontroller.

So, I ported a very simple FORTH model, 328eForth, over to the ATmega328P microcontroller. It was written in AVR assembly language, and had to be assembled in the AVR Studio 4 IDE from Atmel Corp, and then uploaded to ATmega328P through a separated AVRISP mkll programming cable. Once 328eForth is uploaded to ATmega328P, it can communicate with the PC through the Arduino USB cable. BUT, 328eForth cannot be uploaded through the USB cable, because Arduino 0022 requires a bootloader pre-loaded in thr ATmega328P to upload sketches, and 328eForth must use the bootloader section of flash memory in ATmega328P to store commands which writes new code into the application section of the flash memory at run-time.

For the serious FORTH programmer, a 328eForth system gives you the ultimate control over the ATmega328P microcontroller. For the much larger Arduino user community, we need a FORTH implementation which is compatible with the Arduino 0022 system. Here is my solution: **ceForth_328**. It is written in C as a sketch. It can be compiled and uploaded by Arduino 0022. Once it is uploaded to the Atmega328P microcontroller, it communicates with the PC through the Arduino USB cable.

However, new FORTH commands are compiled only into the RAM memory in ATmega328P. You have only about 1.5 KB of RAM memory to store new commands, and when you turn off Arduino Uno, these new commands are lost.

In spite of these limitations, ceForth_328 is still a very useful system.

You can learn FORTH and use if to evaluate Arduino Uno for various applications. You can also use it to learn about the ATmega328P microcontroller, because it allows you to read and to write all the IO registers.

I specifically added the two commands **PEEK** and **POKE** to read and write RAM memory, which includes all the IO registers. The AVR Family Data Book is a huge 566 page document, and the best way to read it is opening one chapter on an I/O device, reading the register descriptions, using PEEK to look at a register, and using POKE the change the register.

Note 1: At the time when this documentation was written, the Arduino nano was probably not available yet. But this sketch works on both. Tested it myself on UNO and on nano - J.P.

Note 2: Some screen shots show 57 600 at the top. Do not get confused – it runs at 115k as described.

Note 3: For the moment we have put the sketch for download and some more data in my dropbox at
https://www.dropbox.com/sh/2eyn5guey80vx7s/AABAPAty8-0TuY9oPo2jcFd5a?dl=0

The next step will be to have the data and links in ther Forth Wiki of www.Forth-eV.de at
https://wiki.forth-ev.de/doku.php/projects:430eforth:start#arduino_uno_und_arduino_nano

Part One: ceForth_328 for Arduino Uno

1. Introduction

Since 1990, I have been promoting a simple FORTH language model called eForth. This model consists of a kernel of 30 primitive commands which have to be implemented as a list of machine instructions of the host microcontroller, and 190 compound commands constructed from the primitive commands and from other compounded commands.
By isolating machine dependent commands from machine independent commands, the eForth model can be ported to any microcontroller very easily.

This FORTH system, ceForth_328 is derived from the cEF Version 1.0 system written in C, which follows closely the original eForth model, with only 30 primitives. The cEF 1.0 system was compiled by gcc in the cygwin environment. This ceForth_328 is an eForth implementation for the ATmega328P microcontroller from Atmel – here as a sketch on the Arduino 0022 system.

It can be compiled and uploaded to the Arduino Uno Board to give you a taste of FORTH.

Because of the limitations imposed by Arduino 0022, you can add only 1.5 KB of new commands to the RAM memory.
This sounds like a severe limitation. However, because of the compactness of FORTH commands, you can still compile a substantial application into this small RAM memory.
Another serious limitation is that you cannot save the application into the flash memory, because the Arduino 0022 system does not provide tools to write new code to the flash memory at run time.

If you really need to develop large applications and to have the complete control over the underlying microcontroller, you can use the native FORTH system I built for the ATmega328P - the

328eForth system. In this 328eForth system, new FORTH commands are compiled directly into the flash memory, and you can make full use of the 32 KB of flash memory, as well as the 2 KB RAM memory.

The drawback of the native 328eForth system is that you have to have a separate programming device, like **AVRISP mkll**, to upload the code into the flash memory. And it overwrites the Arduino 0022 Bootloader section of the flash memory, so that it can add new commands to the application section of the flash memory.

In essence, 328eForth is not compatible with Arduino 0022. This is the reason why I developed this ceForth_328 system, which is basically a teaser, introducing you to the FORTH language, and perhaps to the real FORTH implementation of 328eForth.

2. From Harvard to Princeton

The first large scale, working computer in the US was the Harvard Mark I, designed by Howard Aiken at Harvard University and built by IBM. It was an electromechanical monster completed in May 1944, with programs stored on paper tape.
Then came ENIAC, built by J. Presper Eckert and John Mauchly at University of Pennsylvania in July 1946. It was based on vacuum tubes, and programmed by patch cords and switches. In these computers, programs were entered through media completely different from mechanisms performing computation, and were called the Harvard Architecture.

In 1945, John von Neumann, then at Princeton University, was invited to visit ENIAC, and then wrote the classic "First Draft of a Report on the EDVAC", in which he proposed **the stored program computer**, where programs and data resided on the same memory medium. It was then called the Princeton Architecture or the von Neumann Architecture, and has been adopted by most computer designers, but not all of them.

The AVR family of microcontrollers from Atmel happened to follow the Harvard Architecture, against the common practice in the industry. The reason was that they use a large flash memory to store programs and a small RAM memory to store data.

The flash memory is organized in 16-bit words and the RAM memory is organized in 8-bit bytes. The two memories are very different in their timing and read/write behaviors, and it warrants two different memory buses and separated instructions to access them.

The Arduino 0022 system used on Arduino boards requires that you write application programs in **'sketches'**, which are based on the C programming language. The C language hides the underlying microcontroller from you. Instead, it presents to you a computing model which is essentially a Harvard Architecture.
Programs are placed in locations hidden from you.
Data are placed in locations you have to declare, and then are secretly assigned by the compiler and the linker.
Functions and data are accessed by assigned names so that you are prevented to make serious mistakes which may cause the computer to crash.
For casual users, Arduino 0022 matches very well with the Atmega328P microcontroller, sharing the same Harvard Architecture, and this undoubtedly is one of the reasons why the Arduinos are such a huge success.

The FORTH programming language definitely belongs to the Princeton Architecture. It assumes that you have free access to all parts of a microcontroller, and that programs and data share the same memory space. Therefore, new commands and new data structures can be added freely so that you have an interactive and extensible system to develop and debug your applications.

The Harvard Architecture in the ATmega328P microcontroller is not a big problem for me. In assembly language, I have the complete control over the instructions, RAM/flash memory spaces, and all the IO devices; and I can impose a FORTH Virtual Machine on the ATmega328 chip. This is 328eForth.

An interesting feature of the ATmega328 is that if you have to write into the application section of the flash memory, that part of your code must reside in the bootloader section of the flash memory. Therefore, I have to take over the bootloader section, and the resulting 328eForth system can not peacefully co-exist with the Arduino 0022 bootloader.

In the Silicon Valley Forth Interest Group, we have had very active discussions on Arduino in the monthly meetings over the years. I was challenged to build an Arduino 0022 compatible FORTH system.

My first response was that I could only build a FORTH language interpreter on Arduino. I could not build a FORTH compiler, because Arduino 0022 would not let me write new code into the flash memory.

So I built a FORTH interpreter on the Arduino Uno Board, and presented it to the SVFIG in the October meeting.

One member suggested: "Why don't you use the RAM memory to store new code? You could not save the compiled new code, but at least you would be able to add new code and exercise it."

Thinking it through, it's not a bad idea. In the ATmega328P, there are 2 KB of RAM, and at least 1.5 KB are free. I cannot store machine instructions in RAM, because ATmega328P only executes machine instructions stored in flash memory.

However, I can design a FORTH Virtual Machine with pseudo instructions, which are pure data as far as ATmega328P is concerned. These pseudo instructions can be stored either in flash or in RAM. All I need is a scheme to unify these two different memories so that I can use the same set of read/write pseudo instructions to read the flash and RAM memories, and to write to the RAM memory.

This is my way of building a Princeton Architecture on a Harvard microcontroller with a Harvard programming language. The FORTH Virtual Machine (FVM) has 30 pseudo instructions as byte codes. The pseudo instructions are written as C routines, and a simple Finite State Machine (FSM), also written in C, executes these byte codes, which can be stored either in the flash or RAM memory.

The complete FORTH operating system, including an interpreter, a compiler and other programming and debugging tools are contained in a big data structure called a dictionary. This dictionary contains a set of records linked into a searchable linked list. Each record is the embodiment of a FORTH command, and consists of
a link field,
a name field and
a code field.

A FORTH command is called externally by a name which is an ASCII string, and internally by a token, which is the address of its code field.

There are two types of FORTH commands:
the primitive commands having lists of pseudo instructions in their code fields,
and the compound commands having lists of tokens in their code fields.

The FORTH dictionary is a large and rather complex data structure, because the name fields and the code fields are of variable length. My very limited experience in C is not sufficient for me to build this data structure in C, although very experienced C programmers in SVFIG assured me that it can be done. I fell back to FORTH to build this dictionary and then imported it into the ceForth_328 sketch as a code array.

The dictionary code array is 8 KB in size, and is allocated and initialized by C in the flash memory. However, the lowest 2304 bytes of this code array is mapped to the RAM memory space in the ATmega328P.

In ATmega328P, the RAM memory space is divided into two parts. The lowest 256 bytes are mapped to the CPU and IO registers, and the rest of the 2048 bytes are RAM memory. The read/write pseudo instructions are smart in that they use RAM memory instructions when the memory address is below 2304, and they use flash memory instructions otherwise. Therefore, the dictionary spans across the flash and RAM memory spaces, so that I can add new commands to the dictionary branch in RAM, while Arduino 0022 thinks I am just writing harmless data into the RAM memory.

This is how you can impose a Princeton Architecture onto a Harvard Architecture.

The limitations are that you have only 1.5 KB to compile new FORTH commands, and that you lose these new commands when you lose power.

As I said before, this ceForth_328 system is a teaser, allowing you to experience FORTH within the confines of Arduino 0022. If you are ready for serious application programming, then you might want to move on to the 328eForth system.

3. What Good is ceForth_328 then?

With the limitations I talked about above, you may ask: "Why should I bother with ceForth_328?"

Well, I had seen lots of discussions in the Arduino community on the Internet and that people missed the PEEK and POKE functions in the BASIC language, that were very popular in the early microprocessor days.

PEEK allows you to examine the contents of a memory location, and

POKE allows you to change the contents at this memory location. They are very useful in debugging an application, especially if the IO registers are mapped into the memory space.

I give you PEEK and POKE in ceForth_328. Here are a few examples to show you what you can do with PEEK and POKE.

I assume that you have your Arduino Board set up and connected to your PC through the USB cable. I use an Arduino Uno.

First bring up Arduino 0022,
and click the **File/Open** button;
then select the **ceForth_328.pde file**, wherever you last left it.
Compile and **Upload** it to Arduino Uno.
The Arduino window looks like this:

IMPORTANT:

It seems that over time requirements have changed, and

And additional

    constant

is needed where the error message shows.

The download from the Forth-ev Wiki contains this modification already.

Then open **HyperTerminal** for example, and configure it to **115,200 baud, 1 start bit, 8 data bits, 1 stop bit, no parity**, and **no flow control**. You will see the following HyperTerminal console. If not, check to see if you have **the right COM port settings**.

You can use other terminal emulator programs, and I assume that they behave similarly.

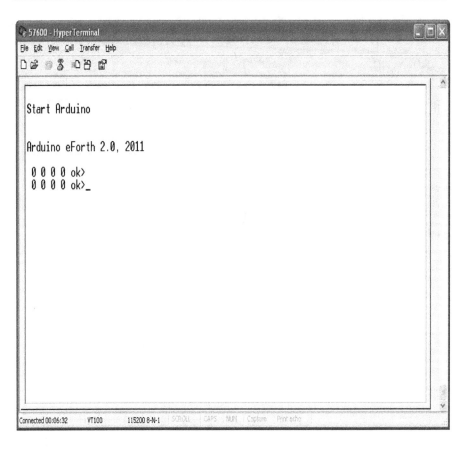

Press the Return key a couple of times, and the **ok>** messages echo on the console.

Type in the following commands to exercise the ceForth_328 system:

```
WORDS
1 2 3 4
+
*
: TEST1 CR ." HELLO, WORLD!" ;
TEST1
: TEST2 IF 1 ELSE 2 THEN . ;
1 TEST2
```

```
0 TEST2
: TEST3 10 FOR R@ . NEXT ;
TEST3
```

ceForth_328 is **NOT case sensitive compared to many other Forths** . You can type commands in either upper or lower case.

Note that ceForth_328 is **in the hexadecimal base** when it starts.

The first time you get an Arduino Board, the first thing you do is to switch that on-board LED on and off.
The LED is connected to the Digital IO Line D13.
With the following POKE commands, you can turn the LED on and off:

```
20   24   POKE
20   23   POKE
20   23   POKE
```

(After POKE, press the **Return key** to send one line of commands to the ATmega328P to be executed.)

The Digital I/O Line D13 on Arduino Uno is connected to
bit-5 of GPIO Port B, PB-5.
Port B is a general purpose I/O device which has the following registers:

Address	Register	Name	Function
$23	PINB	Input register	Status of input pins
$24	DDRB	Direction register	1: output; 0: input
$25	PORTB	Data register	Output data, pull-up resistor

Setting a bit in DDRB register makes the corresponding pin an output pin. This is what the commands

   20 24 POKE

do.

Then, writing this bit in PINB register toggles the output pin. This is done by the commands

   20 23 POKE

The command POKE takes two arguments in front of it:
the first argument is one byte of data, and
the second argument is the address of memory location where the byte data is deposited.

Alternatively, you can POKE the PORTB register to set or clear the bit at PB-5, and respectively turn the LED on or off:

   20   25   POKE
   0   25   POKE

See? When you can poke the IO registers, you can control the ATmega328P chip directly, without writing a sketch.

Type the above commands. Press the Enter key at the end of each line.

You will see how ceForth_328 responds to your commands as shown in the following console display:

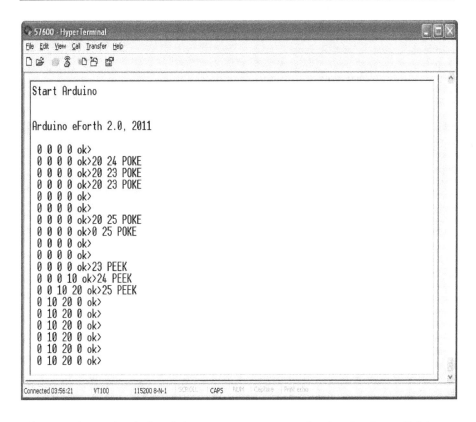

```
57600 - HyperTerminal
File  Edit  View  Call  Transfer  Help

Start Arduino


Arduino eForth 2.0, 2011

0 0 0 0 ok>
0 0 0 0 ok>20 24 POKE
0 0 0 0 ok>20 23 POKE
0 0 0 0 ok>20 23 POKE
0 0 0 0 ok>
0 0 0 0 ok>
0 0 0 0 ok>20 25 POKE
0 0 0 0 ok>0 25 POKE
0 0 0 0 ok>
0 0 0 0 ok>
0 0 0 0 ok>23 PEEK
0 0 0 10 ok>24 PEEK
0 0 10 20 ok>25 PEEK
0 10 20 0 ok>
0 10 20 0 ok>
0 10 20 0 ok>
0 10 20 0 ok>
0 10 20 0 ok>
0 10 20 0 ok>

Connected 03:56:21    VT100    115200 8-N-1    SCROLL    CAPS    NUM    Capture    Print echo
```

The zero's to the left of the prompt **ok>** at the beginning of this session show the top 4 elements on the parameter stack of the FORTH Virtual Machine.

After you execute the commands

23 PEEK

the value returned from register 23 is pushed onto the parameter stack as the number 10.

Subsequently, the value returned by commands

24 PEEK

is 20, and that returned by

25 PEEK

is 0.

You can use PEEK to see the contents of any memory location, including all of the CPU registers, all the IO registers, all the RAM memory, and all the flash memory.
You can use POKE to change the contents of registers and RAM memory. You cannot change the contents of flash memory, though.

Type in the above command lines to verify that you get the same results as shown in the above console display.

Just these two commands PEEK and POKE, make it worthwhile for you to look at ceForth_328 seriously.

Now. Heed this warning!

Use the POKE command carefully.
There is no protection against your poking into sensitive locations which might cause trouble.
You have to stay away, absolutely and positively, from locations 0 to $1F (decimal 0-31), because they map directly into the CPU registers. Only God knows what data is stored there, and they change dynamically.
You are encouraged to poke into the IO registers from $20 to $FF, but you have to study carefully the AVR Family Data Book so that you know exactly what the consequences are, before you try it.
If you do the poking correctly, you can make all the IO devices do what you want. However, incorrectly poking the IO register may have no ill consequences, or may crash the system at the worst.

The C compiler uses RAM locations from $100 to $2FF. ceForth_328 uses the RAM locations from $300 to $8FF.
If you did not compile new commands into the RAM memory, locations from $380 to $87F are free, and you can poke these locations without any problem.

PEEK allows you to examine memory contents - one byte at a time.
I give you a much more powerful command **DUMP** to display 256 bytes of contiguous memory locations. **DUMP** takes one argument as an address, and displays the contents of the next 256 bytes in a nicely formatted table. For example, the command

  0 **DUMP**

displays the contents of all the CPU registers and all the IO registers, as shown in the following:

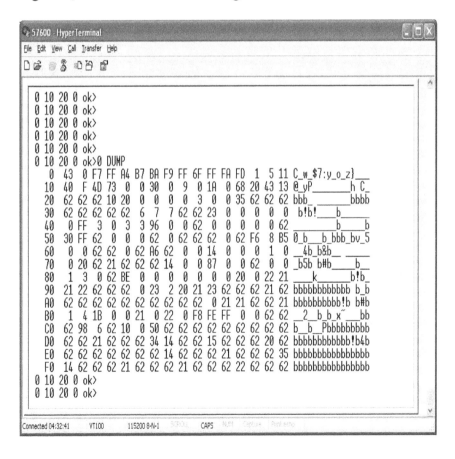

Here, you see the contents of the CPU registers from location 0 to $1F, and those of the IO registers from $20 to $FF. The locations showing data of $62 are those not implemented as IO registers. The locations showing data other than $62 are generally valid registers. Poke them carefully after you study their functions in the AVR Family Data Book. ceForth_328 is the best companion of the AVR Family Data Book as you read about the ATmega328 microcontroller.

Another example is the commands

900 DUMP

and the results are shown in the following:

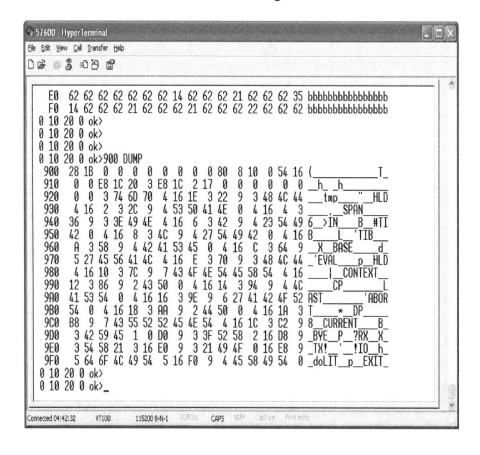

It shows the first 256 bytes of the ceForth_328 dictionary with 19 complete records of FORTH commands. The data dumped in bytes may not make any sense to you at this point, but you should recognize the names of these commands in the ASCII dump on the right hand side of the display.

The dictionary covers the flash memory locations from $900 to $1C9B. You can POKE or DUMP this area at will. You cannot change the contents and POKE has no effect on them.

Do you like PEEK and POKE? As a matter of fact, PEEK and POKE are actually aliases of the commands C@ and C!, which are native FORTH command common to most FORTH systems. It is kind of cheating, but I hope you are a good sport.

4. FORTH Virtual Machine

A FORTH Virtual Machine (FVM) is a program which makes a real microcontroller behave like a FORTH language processor. The FVM has a set of pseudo instructions which supports the primitive FORTH commands and also the token lists in the compound FORTH commands. All FORTH commands operate on parameters stored on a parameter stack. Compound commands use a separated return stack to process nested token lists.

The ceForth_328 FVM is implemented as a Arduino sketch in a file named ceForth_328.pde. It is compiled by Arduino 0022 compiler and the results are uploaded to Arduino Uno for execution. Here I will go through the source code in ceForth_328.pde to explain how this FVM works.

4.1. FORTH Virtual Machine in C

The source code is in ceForth_328.pde. It is compiled as a sketch by Arduino 0022. The first section has a set of macros as #define statements:

```
#include <avr/pgmspace.h>
#define LOGICAL ? 0xFFFF: 0
#define LOWER(x,y) ((unsigned
    int)(x)<(unsigned int)(y))
#define pop top = *S—
#define push *++S = top; top =
#define data      ((unsigned int*) (0))
#define cData     ((unsigned char*) (0))
```

We have to include avr/pgmspace.h library to access arrays in the flash memory.

The following macros are defined to simply coding.

Macro	Function
LOGICAL	Return a -1 for TRUE condition and a 0 for FALSE condition.
LOWER	Used by UM+ pseudo instruction to generate a carry.
push	Push the contents in the top register to the parameter stack.
pop	Pop the parameter stack back into the top register.
data	Pointer to the RAM memory space to access 16-bit data.
cData	Pointer to the RAM memory space to access byte data.

We need to access directly the entire physical RAM memory space, and the mechanism to do it is in declaring two macros data and cData as shown in above.

Declaration of FVM data registers and arrays include the following

```
unsigned char* cCode;
int n;
int  I, P, IP, top ;
unsigned char I1, I2;
int w, clock;
int phase;
int rack[32] = {0};
int stack[32] = {0};
int* R = rack;
int* S = stack;
int code[] PROGMEM = {
```

The functions of these registers and arrays are listed below:

Register/Array	Functions
I	Instruction latch
P	Program counter, pointing to pseudo instructions in code[].
IP	Interpreter pointer for address interpreter
top	Top elements of the parameter stack
I1	Instruction register for the first byte code in a 16 bit word
I2	Instruction register for the second byte code in a 16 bit word
clock	Clocking register for a 4 phase clock in FVM
phase	Phase register
n	Scratch register

w	Scratch register
rack	Return stack
stack	Data stack
R	Return stack pointer
S	Data stack pointer
cCode	A byte pointer to access eForth dictionary in bytes
code	An 8 Kbytes array to host eForth dictionary

Contents of the code array is generated by a separated FORTH program **called a metacompiler**. It is discussed in Part Two of this manual. This code array is placed in the flash memory by the attribute PROGMEM. Special functions in the pgmspace.h library file are called to address this array in the flash memory.

4.2. FORTH Finite State Machine

Skip over the code array, and we have the familiar Arduino routines of setup() and loop(). loop() is the Finite State Machine (FSM) in FVM to execute pseudo instructions stored in the code array.

```
  void setup()
{
    Serial.begin(115200);
    clock = 0;
    P = pgm_read_word(&code[0x480]);
    IP = 0;
    S = stack;
    R = rack;
    top = 0;
    phase = 0;
    cCode = (unsigned char *) code;
    Serial.println("");
```

```
        Serial.println("Start Arduino");
        Serial.println("");
}
```

`setup()` initializes all the registers in FVM. It also initializes the USART0 to 115,200 bauds, and displays a sign-on message. The program counter is initialized to an address stored in the flash memory location $900. As a 16 bit word is fetched out of this location, the actual word address is $480, half of $900. This address points to the FORTH command `COLD` at location $1ACC, which further initializes the FVM and then starts the FORTH interpreter.

The routine `loop()` is a Finite State Machine (FSM) as computer hardware designers would call it.

```
void loop()
{ phase = clock & 3;
    switch(phase) {
        case 0: fetch_decode(); break;
        case 1: execute(I1); break;
        case 2: execute(I2); break;
        case 3: jump(); break;
        }
    clock += 1;

}
```

The simplicity of `loop()` is deceptive. It is an infinite loop, and every cycle through it is a FSM clock cycle, and the `clock` register is incremented. The least significant two bits in the `clock` register is copied into the `phase` register, which runs the 4-state FSM. In Phase 0, `fetch_code` fetches a new program word from a location pointed to by the P register, and the two byte codes in this program word are stored into I1 and I2 registers. In the next cycle, the `phase` register is 1, and in Phase 1, the byte code in I1 is executed by the routine `execute(I1)`. In the next cycle, execute(I2) does just that, executing the byte code in I2. In Phase 3, the routine jump() does nothing and the FSM is ready to go to Phase0 to fetch the next program word.

This simple FSM executes all primitive FORTH commands which contain pseudo instructions in their code fields. As we will see later, a special pseudo instruction dolist which is the first byte in the code field of a compound FORTH command, starts processing a nested list of tokens.

There are two versions of loop(). The one I show above is the regular one. The second one is for debugging. You may need it when you make changes to the code, or to the dictionary in the code array. Using this version, you can single step through the code, and observe changes in the registers and in the stacks. It was very helpful for me in developing this sketch. I only commented this part out, in case you will need it when you revise this sketch and start crashing the system.

```
void loop()
{    phase = clock & 3;
     if ( Serial.available()>0 )
     {
        n = Serial.read();
        switch(phase) {
           case 0: fetch_decode(); break;
           case 1: execute(I1); break;
           case 2: execute(I2); break;
           case 3: jump(); break;
           }
        Serial.println(n, HEX);
        Serial.print("clock=");
        Serial.print(clock,HEX);
        Serial.print(" IP=");
```

```
            Serial.print(IP,HEX);
            Serial.print(" P=");
            Serial.print(P,HEX);
            Serial.print(" I=");
            Serial.print(I,HEX);
            Serial.print(" I1=");
            Serial.print(I1,HEX);
            Serial.print(" I2=");
            Serial.println(I2,HEX);
            dumpStack();
                clock += 1;
            }
}
void dumpStack(void)
{ int n;
  Serial.print("S=" );
  for ( n = 0; n <= (S-stack) ;
n++ )
  { Serial.print(stack[n],HEX);
    Serial.print(" "); }
  Serial.println(top,HEX );
  Serial.print("R=" );
  for ( n = 0; n <= (R-rack) ; n++
)
  { Serial.print(rack[n],HEX);
    Serial.print(" "); }
  Serial.println("");
}
```

DumpStack displays the contents of the parameter stack with the top register, and the return stack.

4.3. Pseudo Instructions

Following are the routines which implement the pseudo instructions in the FVM.

```
void jump(void) { clock |= 3; }
void fetch_decode(void)
{ if ( P < 0x900) { I = data[P>>1];
}
  else { I = pgm_read_word(&code[P>>1]);
}
  P += 2;
  I1= (unsigned char) (I & 0xFF);
  I2= (unsigned char) (I >> 8 );
} void next(void)
{ if ( IP < 0x900) { P = data[IP>>1]; }
  else { P = pgm_read_word(&code[IP>>1]);
}
  IP += 2; jump(); }
void bye() { exit(0); }
```

Instruction	Function
jump	It sets the two least significant bits in the clock register, and forces the next phase to Phase 0 in the next execution cycle, to fetch the next program word. If jump is executed in Phase 1, the byte code which would be execute in Phase 2 is skipped.
fetch_decode	It is always executed in Phase 0. It fetches the next program word pointed to by P, decode the bytes codes in this word and stores them in I1 and I2 registers. The program word can be in the flash memory or in the RAM memory. Since the program word is a 16-bit integer, the program pointer P must be divided by 2, and the word is fetched using word arrays data or code.

next	Inner Interpreter. It terminates all primitive FORTH commands. When FORTHis running, it is always interpreting or processing a token list in a compound FORTH command. The interpreter pointer IP is always pointing to the next token in that token list. `next` fetches the token pointed to by IP, and store it in the program counter P. IP is incremented, pointing to the next token to be processed. Then, `jump` is called to execute the first word in this token. If this token points to a primitive FORTH command, the pseudo instructions in its code field are executed in sequence, until the `next` at the end. If this token points to a compound FORTH command, the first pseudo code to be executed is `dolist`, causing the following token list to be nested and processed.
bye	It is used to terminate a C program and return to the host operating system. In embedded system, you have no place to return and `bye` is not used.

```
void qrx(void)
  { if (Serial.available() == 0) { push
0; }
    else { push Serial.read(); push
OxFFFF; }
  }
void txsto(void) { Serial.write(
(char)
   top); pop; }
void emit(void) { txsto(); }
void docon(void)
{ if ( P < 0x900) { push data[P>>1]; }
  else { push pgm_read_word(&code[P>>1]);
}
  P += 2; }
void dolit(void)
{ if ( IP < 0x900) { push data[IP>>1];
}
  else  { push
pgm_read_word(&code[IP>>1]); }
  IP += 2; next(); }
void dolist(void) { *++R = IP;
       IP = P; next(); }
void exitt(void) { IP = *R--; next(); }
void execu(void) { *++R = IP; P = top;
       pop; jump(); }
void donext(void)
  { if(*R) { *R -= 1 ;
    { if ( IP < 0x900) { IP =
data[IP>>1]; }
       else { IP =
          pgm_read_word(&code[IP>>1]);
}
    }}
    else { IP += 2; R-- ; } next(); }
void qbran(void)
  { if(top == 0)
```

```
     { if ( IP < 0x900) { IP = data[IP>>1];
}
       else { IP =
pgm_read_word(&code[IP>>1]);
            }
     }
    else IP += 2; pop; next(); }
void bran(void)
{ if ( IP < 0x900) { IP = data[IP>>1]; }
   else { IP = pgm_read_word(&code[IP>>1]);
}
    next(); }
```

Instruction	Function
qrx	If USART0 receiver receives a character, push it and a TRUE flag on parameter stack. Otherwise, push a FALSE flag on stack.
txsto	Send a character on top of stack to USART0 transmitter.
emit	Same as txsto
docon	Fetch next word pointer to by P and push it on stack. Increment P.
dolit	Fetch next word pointed to by IP and push it on stack. Increment IP.
dolist	Address Interpreter. Push IP on return stack. Copy P into IP, and execute next to start processing this new token list pointed to by the original IP. This pseudo instruction starts a token list in a compound command.
exitt	Pop return stack back to IP. Execute next to continue processing the token list interrupted by a compound command. It terminates a token list.
execu	Push IP on return stack. Pop stack into P, and start executing the pseudo instructions starting at P.

donext	If top of return stack is not 0, decrement it and then copy the next word into IP, thus repeating a loop. If top of return stack is 0, pop it off return stack, and increment IP, leaving this loop.
qbran	If top of stack is 0, copy the next program word into IP, and then execute `next` to branch to a new token list. If top of stack is not 0, just increment IP, and then execute `next` to continue processing the current token list. It is used to start a conditional branch in a token list.
bran	Copy the next program word into IP, and then execute `next` to branch to a new token list.

```
void store(void)
   { data[top>>1] = *S--; pop; }
void cstore(void)
   { cData[top] = (char) *S--; pop; }
void at(void)
{ if ( top < 0x900) { top = data[top>>1];
}
   else { top = pgm_read_word(&code
        [top>>1]); }
   }
void cat(void)
   {   if   (top   <   0x900)   top   =   (int)
cData[top];
     else top = (int)
pgm_read_byte(&cCode[top]); }   void
icat(void) { top = (int) pgm
        _read_byte(&cCode[top]); }
void iat(void)  { top =
        pgm_read_word(&code[top]); }
void istore(void) { pop; pop; }
void icstore(void) { pop; pop; }
void rfrom(void) { push *R--; }
void rat(void) { push *R; }
```

```
void tor(void) { *++R = top; pop; }
void rpsto(void) { R = rack; }
void spsto(void) { S = stack; }
void drop(void) { pop; }
void dup(void) { *++S = top; }
void swap(void) { w = top; top = *S; *S =
w; } void over(void) { push S[-1]; }
void zless(void) { top = (top & 0X8000)
          LOGICAL ; }
void andd(void) { top &= *S--; }
void orr(void) { top |= *S--; }
void xorr(void) { top ^= *S--; }
void uplus(void) { *S += top; top =
          LOWER(*S, top) ; }
void nop(void) { jump(); }
void dovar(void) { push P; }
```

Instruction	Function
store	Store the second element on stack to a location whose address is on top of stack. Pop both elements.
cstore	Store the second element as a byte on stack to a location whose address is on top of stack. Pop both elements.
at	An address is on top of stack. Fetch the contents in this location and store it on top of stack.
cat	An address is on top of stack. Fetch a byte from this location and store it on top of stack.
icat	An address is on top of stack. Fetch a byte from this location in the flash memory and store it on top of stack. Not used in this implementation.

iat	An address is on top of stack. Fetch a word from this location in the flash memory and store it on top of stack. Not used in this implementation.
istore	Store the second element on stack to a location in the flash memory whose address is on top of stack. Pop both elements. Not used in this implementation.
icstore	Store the second element as a byte on stack to a location in the flash memory whose address is on top of stack. Pop both elements. Not used in this implementation.
rfrom	Pop the return stack and push its top element on stack.
rat	Copy the top element on the return stack and push it on stack.
tor	Pop stack and push its top element on return stack.
rpsto	Initialize the return stack.
spsto	Initialize the parameter stack.
drop	Pop the parameter stack.
dup	Duplicate top of stack.
swap	Swap the top two elements on stack.
over	Duplicate and push the second element on stack.
zless	If top of stack is negative, replace it with a TRUE flag; else replace it with a FALSE flag.
andd	Pop top of stack and AND it to the new top element.
orr	Pop top of stack and OR it to the new top element.
xorr	Pop top of stack and XOR it to the new top element.

uplus	Add top two elements on stack, replace them with a double integer sum.
nop	No operation.
dovar	Push the address in P on stack.

In the other implementation 328eForth, I followed the Harvard Architecture of AVR and addressed the RAM memory and flash memory with separated pseudo instructions. The RAM memory was addressed by the pseudo instructions store, cstore, at and cat. The flash memory was addresses by the pseudo instructions istore, icstore, iat and icat. With the new unified memory model of the Princeton Architecture, the pseudo instructions store. cstore, at and cat are enhanced to address both RAM and flash memories. I allocated 8 KB to the code array. The first 2304 bytes are mapped to the RAM memory, and the rest are mapped to the flash memory. This unified memory model allows me to extend the FORTH dictionary in the flash memory to the RAM memory. I use the same FORTH commands to read and write both RAM and flash memory. Of course, I cannot write new code into the actual flash memory, and the write commands do not change contents in the flash memory. Logically, I could write new data into the flash memory, if tools were provided by the Arduino 0022 system.

4.4. Executing Pseudo Instructions

After 33 pseudo instructions are coded in C routines, execution pointers of these 33 instructions are collected in an execution pointer array *primitives[64]. The routine execute uses a byte value code to select and execute one of the 33 pseudo instructions. Only 30 pseudo instructions are actually used.

```
void (*primitives[64])(void) = {
    /* case 0 */ nop,
    /* case 1 */ bye,
    /* case 2 */ qrx,
    /* case 3 */ txsto,
    /* case 4 */ docon,
    /* case 5 */ dolit,
    /* case 6 */ dolist,
    /* case 7 */ exitt,
    /* case 8 */ execu,
    /* case 9 */ donext,
    /* case 10 */ qbran,
    /* case 11 */ bran,
    /* case 12 */ store,
    /* case 13 */ at,
    /* case 14 */ cstore,
    /* case 15 */ cat,
    /* case 16 */ icat,
```

```
      /* case 17 */ iat,
      /* case 18 */ rfrom,
      /* case 19 */ rat,
      /* case 20 */ tor,
      /* case 21 */ dovar,
      /* case 22 */ next,
      /* case 23 */ drop,
      /* case 24 */ dup,
      /* case 25 */ swap,
      /* case 26 */ over,
      /* case 27 */ zless,
      /* case 28 */ andd,
      /* case 29 */ orr,
      /* case 30 */ xorr,
      /* case 31 */ uplus,
      /* case 32 */ icat
};
void execute(unsigned char
icode)
{   if(icode < 33) {
    primitives[icode]();
  } else {
    Serial.println ("");
    Serial.print ("Illegal
code=");
    Serial.print(icode,
HEX) ;
    Serial.print(" P=" ) ;
    Serial.println(P, HEX
) ;
  }
}
```

5. Examples

ceForth_328 has about 1.5 KB of RAM memory free to compile new FORTH commands. It is not very big, but enough to compile substantial applications. Here I will show you a few examples to get you started.

5.1. Compiler Tests

When I implement a new FORTH system, there are a few new commands I always use to test the system, and to verify that the compiler works correctly. These test commands are show in the TESTS.TXT file. Get the Auduino 0022 up and upload ceForth_328.pde. Then get the HyperTerminal up. You will see the HyperTerminal console as follows:

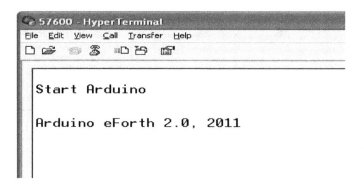

Select Transfer/Transfer Text File and you get a file selection window. Navigate to the folder where ceForth_328 sits, and you see these text files:

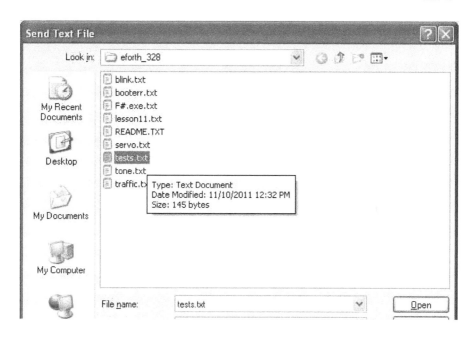

Double click the TESTS.TXT file, and its contents are sent to ceForth_328, as shown in the following:

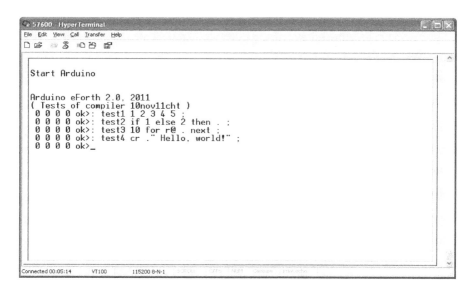

Now, type these commands to test these commands:

```
test1    0 test2    1 test2    test3    test4
```

5.2. BLINK

Blink.pde is generally the first sketch people would try which they first get an Arduino Board. I showed you before how to turn the D13 LED on and off in an earlier section. Here I will show you the FORTH program which blinks the LED. The commands are in the file Blink.txt. Assuming you have the Arduino Board ready with ceForth_328, and with HyperTerminal active, click Transfer/Transfer Text File. In the file selection window, select Blink.txt file, and the following commands are compiled:

```
( Blink Line D13, 01nov11cht)
HEX
: MS ( n -- ) FOR AFT $40 FOR NEXT THEN
NEXT ;
: BLINK 20 24 C! BEGIN 20 23 C! 400 MS ?KEY
UNTIL ;
```

The MS command causes a delay. You give the number of milliseconds before MS.

In the BLINK command, we first initialize the D13 line as an output port, and then fall into an infinite loop.

In the loop, the LED is toggled, and there is a delay by the commands:

```
400 MS
```

400 in hexadecimal is 1024 in decimal. Therefore, the delay lasts about 1000 milliseconds.

After that, ?KEY looks at the USART0 receiver. If there is no input character, the loop is repeated. If you hit any key on the keyboard, the loop will be terminated.

Type in the command BLINK with a Return, the D13 LED will blink. On for 1 second and off for 1 second, until you hit a key, and ceForth_328 returns to the text interpreter, showing the ok> prompt.

5.3. TONE

This example allows you to generate a tone on the **D6 digital output** line. Why D6?
Because D6 connects to one of the outputs from the Timer/Counter0 in ATmega328P. We will thus use Timer/Counter0 to produce a square wave on D6. If you connect one lead of a speaker or a buzzer to D6, and the other lead to the ground, you will hear a tone.

The commands to generate a tone are in the file Tone.txt, as shown below:

```
( Tone generator, 09nov11cht)

HEX
: SETUP
  40 2A C! \ make OC0A (I/O Line 6,
           \ PD-6) an output pin
  42 44 C! \ toggle OC0A on compare match,
           \ select CTC mode
  FF 47 C! \ maximum count in OCR0A
           \ to compare
  3  45 C! \ select /64, prescaler=3,
           \ start counter
  ;
: PRESCALER ( 0-5 -- )
  45 C! ;
: TUNING ( c -- )
  47 c! ;
```

Load this file in HyperTerminal as shown before. Then type in

SETUP

If you had a speaker connected to D6, you will hear a tone.

The Timer/counter0 has a prescaler which scales the master clock and uses the slowed oscillator to drive the counter. The command PRESCALER takes one argument from 0 to 5. Changing the prescaler, you will generate a different tone according to the following table:

Prescaler	Base Frequency
0	Stop oscillator
1	31.2 KHz
2	7.81 KHz
3	980 Hz
4	244 Hz
5	61 Hz

The command TUNING allows you to fine-tune the frequency of the tone more accurately.
TUNING takes one argument from 0 to $FF.
A smaller argument produces a higher pitch.

An exercise you may want to do is to write a command which plays a short song. Use a text editor to edit Tone.txt file. Add some commands to play a song.

5.4. Servo Motors

Are you into robotics? How about using your Arduino Board to drive 6 servo motors?

ATmega328P has three timer/counters. Timer/Counter0 and Timer/Counter2 are 8 bit timer/counters, and Timer/Counter 1 is a 16-bit timer/counter. Timer/Counter1 is more complicated, naturally, but you can run it in the 8-bit mode, so that all three behave similarly. Each Timer/Counter has two outputs which can be programmed to generate two different PWM waves driving two servo motors.

The commands are in the file Servo.txt, as shown below:

```
( Servo Motors on Arduino Uno )
( Chen-Hanson Ting, 5/18/2011
)

( OC1A:   $88,   PB1,   Pin  9    )
( OC1B:   $8a,   PB2,   Pin 10    )
( OC2A:   $b3,   PB3,   Pin 11    )
( OC2B:   $b4,   PD3,   Pin  3    )
( OC0B:   $47,   PD5,   Pin  5    )
( OC0A:   $48,   PD6,   Pin  6    )
( Master clock 16 MHz, prescaler 1024
)
( 3 Counter/Timers, fast PWM mode, )
   ( 8 bit counter   )
( PWM wave frequency 60 Hz, )
   ( period 16 ms    )
( PWM control code: )
   ( $10,  1 ms; $18,  1.5 ms; $20,  2
ms   )
 hex

: init-ports
  E 24 c! 68 2a c! \ output ports
 a3 44 c!  5 45 c! \ TCCR0A, TCCR0B
 18 47 C! 18 48 C! \ OCR0A, OCR0B
 a1 80 c!  d 81 c! \ TCCR1A, TCCR1B
 18 88 c! 18 8a C! \ OCR1A, OCR1B
 a3 b0 c!  7 b1 c! \ TCCR2A, TCCR2B
 18 b3 C! 18 b4 C! \ OCR2A, OCR2B
 ;
```

```
: s1 ( n -- ) 88 c! ;
: s2 ( n -- ) 8a c! ;
: s3 ( n -- ) b3 c! ;
: s4 ( n -- ) b4 c! ;
: s5 ( n -- ) 47 c! ;
: s6 ( n -- ) 48 c! ;
```

The command init-ports is a bit complicated, and you have to read the three chapters in the AVR Family Data Book on Timer/Counter1, 2 and 3 to fully understand it.

However, I just summarized the most important information on these timer/counters in the comment lines at the beginning of Servo.txt file shown above.

Six servo motors are connected to Digital lines D3, D5, D6, D9, D10, and D11.
D3, D5, and D6 are driven by three lines in Port PD as PD3, PD5 and PD6, respectively.
D9, D10, and D11 are driven by three lines in Port PB as PB1, PB2 and PB3, respectively.
The commands in init-ports

E 24 c! 68 2a c! \ output ports

assigned these 6 lines as output lines.

Relevant IO registers, their addresses, and their basic functions are summarized in the following table:

Register	Timer/Counter0	Timer/Counter1	Timer/Counter2	Function
TCCRnA	44	80	B0	Timer control register A
TCCRnB	45	81	B1	Timer

				control register B
OCRnA	47	88	B3	Output compare register A
OCRnB	48	8A	B4	Output compare register B

To drive a servo motor you give it a PWM wave at 50 Hz, with the turn-on period varying from 1 ms to 2 ms. This range is controlled by writing a value from $10 to $20 into the corresponding output compare register. An initial value of $18 written into the output compare registers sets the servo motors at their mid points. The commands S1 to S6 allow you to change the set points of these 6 motors.

If you examine the output lines with an oscilloscope, you will see that the output PWM waves have a frequency of 60 Hz instead of the required frequency of 50 Hz.

This is due to the fact that the ATmega328P is driven by a 16 MHz crystal clock, and 60 Hz comes out the prescalers naturally. If you want to drive servos at exactly 50 Hz, you can use one timer/counter to drive a second one and tune the first timer/counter accurately for 50 Hz operation. But then, you could only drive 3 servo motors. However, most servo motors do not really care about the base frequency of the PWM waves, and 60 Hz works just fine.

5.5. Traffic Controller

A traffic controller is my favorite demo application. I often challenge people to write the simplest and the most efficient program to control traffic lights at a highway intersection. In each of the north, south, east and west directions, I place two sensors to sense forward and left-turn cars, and 4 lights to indicate go, left-turn, caution, and stop signals. On the Arduino Boards, there are not enough output lines to drive 16 traffic signals, so I give the north and south directions the same 4 signals, and the east and west directions another 4 signals.

The commands are in the Traffic.txt file, as shown below:

```
( Traffic Controller on Arduino Uno )
( Chen-Hanson Ting, 5/10/2011         )
( Switches: )
  ( PC: 0, N; 1, NL; 2, S; 3, )
  ( SL; 4, W; 5, WL )
(         PB: 2: E; 3, EL )
( LEDs:   PD: 2, nsG; 3, nsY; 4, nsR, 5,
)
(             nsL; 6, ewG; 7,ewY )
(         PB: 0, ewR; 1,ewL )
  hex

: init-ports
    fc 2a c! 3 24 c!   \ output
ports
    3f 28 c! c 25 c! ; \ input ports,
                       \ pullup
resistors
: seconds for aft 100 for 100 for next
next
    then next ;
: lights ( n -- )
    dup 2b c!                \ PD outputs
    100 / C or 25 c! ;
            \ PB outputs, maintain
pullups

: switches ( -- n )
    23 c@ 100 *   \ PB inputs
    26 c@ or      \ PC inputs
```

```
    dup cr . ;

: N-S begin 104 lights 5 seconds
switches c3a and if 108 lights 2
seconds then  switches a and if 130
lights 3 seconds then  switches c30 and
until
  ;

: E-W begin 50 lights 5 seconds
    switches 82f and if 90 lights
        2 seconds then
    switches 820 and if 310 lights
        3 seconds then
    switches f and until
  ;

: go  init-ports
    begin N-S E-W ?key until drop ;
```

I am very proud of this program, as I have revised it several times
and now it is in its best shape. The IO port assignments are as
follows:

Port	IO Line	IO Device	Function
D2	PD2	Green LED	North-South Go
D3	PD3	Yellow LED	North-South Caution
D4	PD4	Red LED	North-South Stop
D5	PD5	Green LED	North-South Left-Turn
D6	PD6	Green LED	East-west Go
D7	PD7	Yellow LED	East-west Caution
D8	PB0	Red LED	East-west Stop
D9	PB1	Green LED	East-west Left-Turn
A0	PC0	Switch	North Forward

A1	PC1	Switch	North Left-Turn
A2	PC2	Switch	South Forward
A3	PC3	Switch	South Left-Turn
A4	PC4	Switch	West Forward
A5	PC5	Switch	West Left-Turn
D10	PB2	Switch	East Forward
D11	PB3	Switch	East Left-Turn

Commands are explained in the following table:

Command	Function
init-ports	Initialize the three IO ports PA, PC and PD. The input ports do not have to be initialized, except that their pull-up resistors are activated for the proper operation of external switches. It is very satisfying that the ATmega328P can drive LED's directly with its output lines without current limiting resistors, and that it has optional pull-up resistors to simplify input circuitry. The actual layout of the traffic controller is therefore extremely simple.
seconds	Delay a number of seconds.
lights	From a 16 bit value, turn on/off 8 LEDs. The lower byte controls PD port, and the upper byte controls PB port.
switches	From a 16 bit value, read 8 switches. The lower byte reads PC port, and the upper byte controls PB port.
N-S	A loop managing north-south traffic. If either forward switches in the north or south direction are active, turn on North-South Go LED for 5 seconds. Next, if there are activity in other directions, turn on North-South Stop and Caution LEDs for 2 seconds. Then, if either left-

	turn switches in the north or south direction are active, turn on North-South Stop and Left-turn LED for 3 seconds. Then, if there are activity in the East-West direction, turn off North-South Caution LED's and exit this command so that E-W command has a chance to run. Otherwise, repeat N-S loop.
E-W	A loop managing east-west traffic. If either forward switches in the east or west direction are active, turn on East-West Go LED for 5 seconds. Next, if there are activity in other directions, turn on East-West Caution LED for 2 seconds. Then, if either left-turn switches in the east or west direction are active, turn on East-West Stop and Left-turn LEDs for 3 seconds. Then, if there are activity in the East-West direction, turn off East-west Caution LEDs and exit this command so that N-S command has a chance to run. Otherwise, repeat E-W loop.
go	Initialize IO ports and enter a loop repeating N-S and E-W commands. Exit this loop if the user hit any key on the keyboard.

This program is simple because I realized that it is a Finite State Machine with two major states, which are coded as N-S and S-W commands. There are three minor states in either major states, and they are sequenced through under the appropriate conditions. You can treat it as a 6-state Finite State Machine, but the transition rules would be much more complicated.

5.6. More Lessons

There are 17 lessons in files lesson1.txt to lesson17.txt. Take a look at these files and enter the commands as exercises to learn eForth. You can also download these files through the Transfer/Transfer text file button. However, remember that you have only about 1.5 KB of RAM space to compile new commands. When you compile too many commands, ceForth_328 will crash and stop talking to you. Push the reset button on Arduino Uno to start over.

If you think you are about to crash, the can use the command **COLD** to start over, or use the command:

FORGET <name>

to trim the dictionary back to a command you compiled earlier. COLD or FORGET allow you to reclaim the dictionary space so that you can compile more commands.

6. Conclusion

I can bore you to death with more examples, but this seems a good point to stop. What I want to show you is that within the confines of Arduino 0022, it is possible to build a FORTH programming environment to let people explore this simple yet powerful programming language. Although the small RAM memory in ATmega328P limits the number of new commands you can add to the FORTH system, and Arduino 0022 does not allow you to save the commands ceForth_328 compiles, it is a useful environment for you to explore this interesting microcontroller while you are reading the huge 566 page AVR Family Data Book.

PEEK and POKE are aliases of the native FORTH commands C@ and C!. They clearly demonstrate the power and the usefulness of FORTH as a programming language.

ATmega328P is a much more powerful microcontroller than what Arduino 0022 allows it to be. The roots of Arduino 0022 are in the UNIX operating system and in the C programming Language. I admire the developers of Arduino in simplifying the operating system and the language to the point that you are presented with only two routines:

```
setup();
```

```
loop()
```

Most of the complications in the operating system and in the language are hidden from you so that you can go immediately doing useful things. However, the operating system and the language still insulate you from the underlying microcontroller, and prevent you from exploit the microcontroller to its full capacity.

FORTH is an operating system and a programming language which are transparent between you and the microcontroller you own. At the very low end, it allows you to push the microcontroller to the bare metal, giving you complete control over the registers, the IO devices and the memory. At the other end, it allows you to express your programming intentions at the highest conceptual level, in building nested lists to arbitrary depth, much like LISP albeit simpler, easier and without the irritating parentheses.

The ceForth_328 system is a teaser to give you some hands-on experience with FORTH on an Arduino Board. It introduces you to a real FORTH system 328eForth which give you access to the entire ATmega328P microcontroller, and allows you to build complete turnkey applications for Arduino Boards and even for bare ATmega328P chips. I hope to convince you that there is a better way to develop turnkey applications than Arduino 0022.

You see. The Arduino 0022 system comes in a zipped file of 87,587 KB. It expands to fill 245 MB on your hard disk. You really don't know what's happening behind your back when you compile a sketch in Arduino 0022. It always amazes me that the results uploaded to the Arduino Uno Board actually works. It is a long and tedious task to learn about all the library routines provided in the Arduino 0022 system. Very often, it is difficult to find utilities and tools that you need to do your job. The huge Arduino community helps, but only to an extend. You are on your own in the end.

In contrast, the assembly source code of 328eForth system has only 54,472 bytes. This is 1/500th the size of the Arduino 0022 system, and it is within a single person's intelligence. However, this 54 KB of source code, describe a complete operating system , a programming language and a whole bunch of tools embedded inside a microcontroller, independent of a host computer or a supporting operating system. It give you complete freedom in developing your specific applications.

Last but not least, actually, ATmega328P and the AVR family of microcontrollers, in my humble opinion, are great chips but of very poor design. Most microcontroller designers really don't know what they are doing. They just throw things together and called them microcontrollers. Not much thought were really put into the architecture, the instruction sets, and the peripheral devices. There were very few visions behind the microcontroller designs. And, hardware designers really do not understand software. They just throw the chip over the fence, and let software engineers make things work. On this side of the fence, software designers really do not understand software either, and they build clumsy, bulky, inefficient systems, plagued with bugs. So, we get a mess. Microcontrollers can be designed simpler and better, if the designers really understand hardware and software. In this respect, probably you should look at my 32-bit FORTH microcontroller design in eP32. But, that's a different story.

Part Two: Metacompilation of ceForth_328

7. Metacompilation

In 1990, Bill Muench and I developed a very simple FORTH model called eForth and it was ported to 30 some different microprocessors and microcontrollers by many volunteers. A young fellow in Taiwan, Mr. Cheah-shen Yap, ported eForth to Windows to become the weForth system. He further enhanced it and released it as the F# system. It is the simplest FORTH implementations for Windows, but can call all Windows APIs to build very sophisticated applications for a PC.

Most of the eForth systems were written in assembly languages native to the underlying microcontrollers. Because the hardware dependencies were contained in a small set of primitive FORTH commands, eForth is very easy to port. You rewrite the primitive commands in an assembler, provided usually free by the microcontroller manufacturer, and copy the source code of all the compound commands over. A new eForth generally can be built in about 2 weeks.

When I worked with Chuck Moore to develop the MuP21 microcontroller, he wrote a metacompiler in the then very popular FORTH system FPC on a PC, to produce testing routines for the new microcontroller. In MuP21, Chuck designed 25 machine instructions, and these machine instructions matched very well with the primitive commands in eForth. I used Chuck's metacompiler to build an eForth system for MuP21, and it worked quite well. Then I went on developing a series of microcontrollers: P8, P16, and P24, using Chuck's metacompiler to build eForth systems for them. When I moved on to a 32-bit microcontroller, I called it eP32 to remind people that the software for it was eForth.

Recently I implemented eForth using the C language, to give C programmers a taste of the FORTH language and perhaps develop applications based on it. It took me half a year to figure out how to convince C to speak FORTH. These two languages are very different in their architecture, primitive instructions, memory management, syntax, and expressions of arithmetic-logic operations. In the end, I took the hardware design of the eP32 microcontroller, and emulated it in C routines as a FORTH Virtual Machine (FVM).

The primitive FORTH commands are encoded in a set of pseudo instructions in this FVM, and the compound FORTH commands are encoded in a giant data structure call a dictionary. I could not express this rather complicated data structure in C. So, I used Chuck's metacompiler to build it in F#, and then imported it into the C program as a data array. I called it the cEF system.

To build a FORTH system for the Arduino Uno Board, based on the C compiler in Arduino 0022 system; it is natural to port the cEF system over as an Arduino sketch.

The FORTH Virtual Machine (FVM) in cEF was copied into an Arduino sketch. The FORTH dictionary was metacompiled by F#, and imported to the Arduino sketch as a data array. The result is ceForth_328, which runs smoothly on my Arduino Uno now.

In FORTH terminology, a metacompiler is a FORTH program which produces a dictionary as a data array, which can be copied into the memory of a target computer. When the target computer powers up, a FORTH system in the dictionary is booted up, and you can type FORTH commands to interact with it.

The new FORTH system may run on the same platform as the old FORTH system. It may be targeted to a new platform, or to a new microcontroller. The new FORTH system may share a large portion of FORTH code with the old system, hence the term "metacompilation" as in metamorphosis. The metacompiler is very similar to a conventional cross assembler/compiler.

I believe the best way to explain this ceForth_328 system is through its source code in the Arduino sketch and in the metacompiler that produces its dictionary. Going through source code almost line by line, I hope that I can explain the process of producing a FORTH target system on Arduino Uno, and everything that goes into the dictionary which makes the Arduino Uno behave like a FORTH language processor inside the ATmega328P microcontroller.

In Part One of this manual, I went through the C source code in the eForth_328.pde file. Now I will do the same for the ceForth_328 metacompiler. If you are new to FORTH, the source code would look strange. I hope you will bear with me in reading the source code. FORTH is more like English (or Chinese for that matter) than a conventional procedural programming language, and is very easy to get used to. Once you learn to read FORTH code, it will be very easy to write your own FORTH programs.

8. ceForth_328 Metacompiler

As discussed earlier, the FORTH Virtual Machine (FVM) is coded in C, and it is really not very complicated. There are only 33 pseudo instructions, and a Finite State Machine (FSM) which sequencing through these pseudo instructions stored in memory. The complication is in the FORTH dictionary which contains an interpreter, a compiler, many debugging tools, and about 200 FORTH commands, all linked into a linear, searchable dictionary. To really understand this FORTH system and use it to develop applications, you need to know most of these commands, how the dictionary is constructed, and how it is extended when new FORTH commands are added to the dictionary.

The dictionary in ceForth_328 system is built by a metacompiler, which is a FORTH program constructing a new FORTH system for a target microcontroller like Atmega328P. For the ceForth_328 system, I call the metacompiler cefMETA328.

It consists of a set of files loaded into the F# system running on Microsoft Windows. F# is a very simple FORTH system. Though it is very simple, it contains tools to access all of the API services provided by Windows. You can build very elaborate and sophisticated applications on the top of it. cefMETA328 is such an application.

The cefMETA328 metacompiler consists of the following set of files, in addition to the files necessary to run the F# system:

File	Function
F#.exe	F# system to compile ceForth_328
cefMETA328.fex	Maker of ceForth_328 metacompiler
cefMETA328.f	Metacompiler of ceForth_328
cefASM328.f	Assembler of ceForth_328 pseudo code
cefKERN328.f	Kernel of primitive commands
cEF328.f	All compound commands
cefSIM328.f	Simulator of ceForth_328 system
rom.mif	Dictionary of ceForth_328
ceForth_328.pde	ceForth_328 source code in C to run on Arduino 0022.

Several other .f files are necessary for F# to work. Do not delete them. All files are compressed in cefMETA328.zip. Unzip it and put all the files in a folder, for example ..\ceForth_328\. Don't leave that folder on your desktop. You must not have spaces in the pathname of this folder.

ceForth_328.pde describes a FORTH Virtual Machine (FVM) in C code. This FVM has a set of pseudo instructions and some C functions to execute FORTH pseudo instructions as a Finite State Machine (FSM). These pseudo instructions are encoded in one byte, and are called byte codes.

The C routines were a discussion in the first part of this manual.

A dictionary allocates an 8 KB code array to host the dictionary of the ceForth_328 system. FORTH commands are coded as records in a single linked list. Each command record has 3 fields:

Field	Function
link field	Points to name field of prior command. 2 bytes.
name field	Counted string of a name. Variable length
code field	Pseudo instructions and token lists. Variable length

In a **primitive command**, the code field has a list of pseudo instructions, terminated by the inner interpreter instruction next,.

In a **constant**, the code field contains two pseudo instructions inline, and next,, which returns the constant value stored in the following program word.

In a **variable**, the code field contains two pseudo instructions dovar, and next,, which returns the address of the following word. This behavior is shared with arrays defined by CREATE.

In a **compound command**, the code field has one pseudo instruction dolist, followed by a token list which is a list of code field addresses of other FORTH commands. It is usually terminated by a FORTH command EXIT, which un-nests a nested token list started by dolist.

The token list in a compound command usually is a linear list of addresses. A number of structures can be embedded in this list, such as:
Literals to return an inline constant
String literals to return the address of an embedded inline string
Control structures for branching and looping

33 pseudo instructions are implemented in this system. Only 30 are actually used.

Up to 256 pseudo instructions can be accommodated in this design. The number of compound commands is limited by the space in the flash memory. An eForth system generally has about 200 compound commands to begin with. You add more to build applications.

Load cefMETA328.fex under F# to build the eForth dictionary. It produces a file rom.mif which contains the hexadecimal image of the ceForth_328 Forth dictionary. Contents of rom.mif must be copied into the `code` memory array in the ceForth_328.pde file to be compiled by Arduino 0022.

The step by step procedure to build and test ceForth_328 is as follows:

1. Power-up Windows XP
2. Unzip all files in ceForth_328.zip into a folder like ..\ceForth_328 \.
3. Double click F#.exe, and bring up a file selection window:

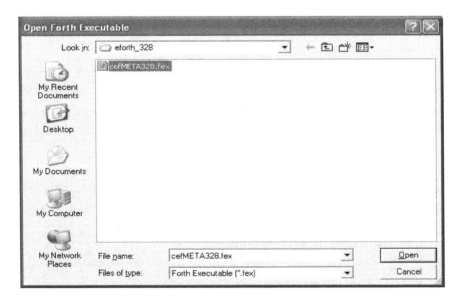

4. Double click cefMETA328.fex in the file selection window. The ceForth_328 metacompiler compiles ceForth_328 and produces a rom.mif file. A ceForth_328 simulator is also loaded and the ceForth_328 system can be simulated.

```
C:\C-EFORTH\leforth_328\F#.exe   Current dir-C:\C EFORTH\leforth_328
File  Edit  Tools  Help
Name Compiler
 ?UNIQUE 17BE reDef ?UNIQUE $,n 17EA reDef $,n
FORTH Compiler
 $COMPILE 181E reDef $COMPILE OVERT 1852 reDef OVERT ; 1862 reDef ; ] 1874 reDef ] : 1884 reDef :
Defining Words
 CODE 189C reDef CODE CREATE 18B0 reDef CREATE VARIABLE 18C8 reDef VARIABLE CONSTANT 18E0 reDef CONSTANT
Tools
 dm+ 18F4 reDef dm+ DUMP 191C reDef DUMP
 >NAME 194A reDef >NAME .ID 197C reDef .ID SEE 19AA reDef SEE WORDS 19F4 reDef WORDS FORGET 1A1A reDef FORGET
DIAGNOSE 1A4C
Hardware reset
 COLD 1B28 reDef COLD
Structures
 <MARK 1B64 <RESOLVE 1B76 >MARK 1B84 >RESOLVE 1B9C
 FOR 1BAC reDef FOR BEGIN 1BBE reDef BEGIN NEXT 1BCC reDef NEXT UNTIL 1BDE reDef UNTIL
 AGAIN 1BF0 reDef AGAIN IF 1C00 reDef IF AHEAD 1C12 reDef AHEAD REPEAT 1C26 reDef REPEAT
 THEN 1C36 reDef THEN AFT 1C42 reDef AFT ELSE 1C56 reDef ELSE WHEN 1C68 WHILE 1C78 reDef WHILE
compilers
 ABORT" 1C8A reDef ABORT" $" 1C9A reDef $" ." 1CAA reDef ."
 .( 1CBA reDef .( \ 1CCA reDef \ ( 1CDA reDef ( IMMEDIATE 1CF2 reDef IMMEDIATE

$ >
 900
 90A
 Loading cefSIM328.F reDef BREAK reDef RESET
$ >
$ >
Version FIX 14jan11CHT
$ > |
```

If you scroll back the console window to the very beginning, you can see all the files being loaded by the F# system. You can see the following commands in the cefMETA328.fex file:

```
FLOAD .\init.f          \ initial stuff
FLOAD .\win32.f         \ win32 system interface
FLOAD .\consolei.f      \ api and constant defination
FLOAD .\ui.f            \ user interface helper routine
                        \ ( reposition )
FLOAD .\console.f       \ the main program
FLOAD .\ansi.f
FLOAD .\fileinc.f
FLOAD .\cefMETA328.f
```

cefMETA328.fex is similar to a MAKE file in UNIX. It first loads in a set of Windows utility files. The last thing cefMETA328.fex file does is to load the cefMETA328.f file, which is the ceForth_328 metacompiler.

We will read the source code in cefMETA329.f later. Here I just summarize the other files loaded by it and what is accomplished by loading these files.

File	Functions
cefMETA328.f	Load cefASM328.f to bring up the ceForth_328 assembler. It prints out a list of command names followed by a reDef message. These commands are the ceForth_328 assembler, preparing to assemble the primitive commands in the ceForth_328 kernel.
cefKERN328.f	First define many system variables starting at target memory location $920. Then it assembles about 30 primitive commands which are the kernel of ceForth_328. There you can see names of target commands followed by their code field addresses. They form a symbol table, which you can use to look up names and addresses of target commands.
cEF328.f	Compile the compound commands which form the bulk of ceForth_328 target system.
cefSIM328.f	ceForth_328 simulator. This simulator faithfully simulate the ceForth_328 system cycle by cyle, instruction by instruction.

Once the cefSIM328.f simulator is loaded, type the command:
HELP

and a list of simulator commands appears.

```
C:\C-FFORTH\eforth_328\F#.exe   Current dir=C:\C-FFORTH\eforth_328
File Edit Tools Help
DIAGNOSE 1A4C
Hardware reset
 COLD 1B28 reDef COLD
Structures
 <MARK 1B64 <RESOLVE 1B76 >MARK 1B84 >RESOLVE 1B9C
 FOR 1BAC reDef FOR BEGIN 1BBE reDef BEGIN NEXT 1BCC reDef NEXT UNTIL 1BDE reDef UNTIL
 AGAIN 1BF0 reDef AGAIN IF 1C00 reDef IF AHEAD 1C12 reDef AHEAD REPEAT 1C26 reDef REPEAT
 THEN 1C36 reDef THEN AFT 1C42 reDef AFT ELSE 1C56 reDef ELSE WHEN 1C68 WHILE 1C78 reDef WHILE
compilers
 ABORT" 1C8A reDef ABORT" $" 1C9A reDef $" ." 1CAA reDef ."
 .( 1CBA reDef .( \ 1CCA reDef \ ( 1CDA reDef ( IMMEDIATE 1CF2 reDef IMMEDIATE

$ >
 900
 90A
 Loading cefSIM328.F reDef BREAK reDef RESET
$ >
$ >
Version FIX 14jan11CHT
$ > HELP
cEF Simulator, copyright Offete Enterprises, 2009
C: execute next cycle
S: show all registers
D: display next 8 words
addr M: display 128 words from addr
addr G: run and stop at addr
RUN: execute, one key per cycle

$ >
```

5.   Type -1 G, and the simulator displays:
Arduino eForth 2.0, 2011

```
C:\C-EFORTH\eforth_328\F#.exe   Current dir=C:\C-EFORTH\eforth_328
File  Edit  Tools  Help
 .( 1CBA reDef .( \ 1CCA reDef \ ( 1CDA reDef ( IMMEDIATE 1CF2 reDef IMMEDIATE
$ >
 900
 90A
  Loading cefSIM328.F reDef BREAK reDef RESET
$ >
$ >
Version FIX 14jan11CHT
$ > HELP
cEF Simulator, copyright Offete Enterprises, 2009
C: execute next cycle
S: show all registers
D: display next 8 words
addr M: display 128 words from addr
addr G: run and stop at addr
RUN: execute, one key per cycle

$ > -1 G
Press any key to stop.

Arduino eForth 2.0, 2011

  0 0 0 0 ok>
  0 0 0 0 ok>
  0 0 0 0 ok>
  0 0 0 0 ok>
  0 0 0 0 ok>
  0 0 0 0 ok>
```

6. Press the return key and the system displays:

0 0 0 0 ok>

7. You can type in other FORTH commands to test the system in the simulator.

Now you can exercise ceForth_328 by typing in FORTH commands.
The following console window shows the results when you type the command:

WORDS

If you care to count them, there are about 195 commands. These commands are documented in the Appendix.

ceForth_328 is case insensitive. You can type in commands in upper case or lower case characters. You can also type in mixed case characters.

```
C:\C-EFORTH\eforth_328\F#.exe  Current dir-C:\C-EFORTH\eforth_328
File Edit Tools Help
S: show all registers
D: display next 8 words
addr M: display 128 words from addr
addr G: run and stop at addr
RUN: execute, one key per cycle

$ > -1 G
Press any key to stop.

Arduino eForth 2.0, 2011

 0 0 0 0 ok>
 0 0 0 0 ok>
 0 0 0 0 ok>
 0 0 0 0 ok>
 0 0 0 0 ok>
 0 0 0 0 ok>WORDS
 IMMEDIATE ( \ .( ." $" ABORT" WHILE WHEN ELSE AFT THEN REPEAT AHEAD IF AGAIN UNTIL NEXT BEGIN
FOR >RESOLVE >MARK <RESOLVE <MARK COLD DIAGNOSE FORGET WORDS SEE .ID >NAME DUMP dm+ CONSTANT VARIABLE
CREATE CODE : ] ; OVERT $COMPILE $,n ?UNIQUE $," LITERAL COMPILE [COMPILE] , ALLOT ' QUIT EVAL
.OK [ $INTERPRET ERROR abort" ABORT QUERY EXPECT accept kTAP TAP ^H NAME? find SAME? NAME> WORD
TOKEN PACK$ CHAR PARSE (parse) ? . U. U.R .R ."| $"| do$ CR TYPE SPACES CHARS SPACE ?KEY NUMBER?
DIGIT? >UPPER UPPER DECIMAL HEX str #> SIGN #S # HOLD <# EXTRACT DIGIT ERASE FILL CMOVE @EXECUTE
TIB PAD HERE COUNT 2@ 2! +! ALIGNED >CHAR BL 2/ 2* 2+ 2- 1+ 1- */ */MOD M* * UM* / MOD /MOD
M/MOD UM/MOD WITHIN MIN MAX < U< = 0= ABS - DNEGATE NEGATE NOT + 2DUP 2DROP ROT ?DUP EMIT KEY
?KEY doVAR doCON doLIST UM+ XOR OR AND 0< OVER SWAP DUP DROP >R R@ R> PEEK POKE IC@ IC! I@ I!
C@ C! @ ! doNEXT BRANCH QBRANCH EXECUTE EXIT doLIT !IO TX! ?RX BYE CURRENT DP 'ABORT LAST CP
CONTEXT HLD 'EVAL BASE 'TIB #TIB >IN SPAN HLD tmp
 0 0 0 0 ok>
```

Here a some more eForth commands you can type into the F#
console to test the eForth system:

```
900 DUMP
HERE .
1 2 + .
: TEST1 1 2 3 4 5 ;
TEST1
: TEST2 10 FOR R@ . NEXT ;
TEST2
: TEST3 IF 1 ELSE 2 THEN . ;
  0  TEST3
  1  TEST3
```

```
: TEST4 CR ." HELLO, WORLD!" ;
TEST4
```

After these tests, the F# console looks as follows.

```
C:\C-EFORTH\eforth_328\F#.exe   Current dir=C:\C-EFORTH\eforth_328
File Edit Tools Help
  900  28 1B  0  0  0  0  0  0  0  0 80  8 10  0 54 16  (             T_
  910   0  0 E8 1C 20  3 E8 1C  2 17  0  0  0  0  0  0 _h  h
  920   0  0  3 74 6D 70  4 16 1E  3 22  9  3 48 4C 44 _tmp     "_HLD
  930   4 16  2  3 2C  9  4 53 50 41 4E  0  4 16  4  3 ___,_SPAN
  940  36  9  3 3E 49 4E  4 16  6  3 42  9  4 23 54 49 6_>IN    B_#TI
  950  42  0  4 16  8  3 4C  9  4 27 54 49 42  0  4 16 B      L_'TIB
  960   A  3 58  9  4 42 41 53 45  0  4 16  C  3 64  9 _X_BASE     d_
  970   5 27 45 56 41 4C  4 16  E  3 70  9  3 48 4C 44 'EVAL___p_HLD
  980   4 16 10  3 7C  9  7 43 4F 4E 54 45 58 54  4 16 ___|_CONTEXT_
  990  12  3 86  9  2 43 50  0  4 16 14  3 94  9  4 4C     CP       L
  9A0  41 53 54  0  4 16 16  3 9E  9  6 27 41 42 4F 52 AST      'ABOR
  9B0  54  0  4 16 18  3 AA  9  2 44 50  0  4 16 1A  3 T     *_DP
  9C0  B8  9  7 43 55 52 52 45 4E 54  4 16 1C  3 C2  9 8_CURRENT   B_
  9D0   3 42 59 45  1  0 D0  9  3 3F 52 58  2 16 D8  9 _BYE_P_?RX_X_
  9E0   3 54 58 21  3 16 E0  9  3 21 49 4F  0 16 E8  9 _TX!_`_!IO_h_
  9F0   5 64 6F 4C 49 54  5 16 F0  9  4 45 58 49 54  0 _doLIT_p_EXIT_
0 0 0 0 ok>HERE . 320
0 0 0 0 ok>1 2 + . 3
0 0 0 0 ok>: TEST1 1 2 3 4 5 ;
0 0 0 0 ok>TEST1
2 3 4 5 ok>: TEST2 10 FOR R@ . NEXT ;
2 3 4 5 ok>TEST2 10 F E D C B A 9 8 7 6 5 4 3 2 1 0
2 3 4 5 ok>: TEST3 IF 1 ELSE 2 THEN . ;
2 3 4 5 ok>0 TEST3 2
2 3 4 5 ok>1 TEST3 1
2 3 4 5 ok>: TEST4 CR ." HELLO, WORLD!" ;
2 3 4 5 ok>TEST4
HELLO, WORLD!
 2 3 4 5 ok>
```

8. Close F# window.

You are done with cefMETA328 metacompiler. It produces a rom.mif file, which contains the dictionary of ceForth_328. You must import this dictionary into the ceForth_328.pde file to get ceForth_328 to work on the Arduino Uno Board.

9. Move ceForth_328 to Arduino Uno

The step by step procedure to get ceForth_328 running on Arduino Uno Board is as follows:
1.   Open Arduino 0022 in Windows.
2.   Open ceForth_328.pde file Arduino 0022.
3.   Copy rom.mif to `code` array in ceForth_328.pde.
Remember to remove the comma at the end of the line

```
/* 1FFE */ 0x0000
```

The Arduino screen should look like the following:

```
/* 1FE0 */ 0x0000,
/* 1FE2 */ 0x0000,
/* 1FE4 */ 0x0000,
/* 1FE6 */ 0x0000,
/* 1FE8 */ 0x0000,
/* 1FEA */ 0x0000,
/* 1FEC */ 0x0000,
/* 1FEE */ 0x0000,
/* 1FF0 */ 0x0000,
/* 1FF2 */ 0x0000,
/* 1FF4 */ 0x0000,
/* 1FF6 */ 0x0000,
/* 1FF8 */ 0x0000,
/* 1FFA */ 0x0000,
/* 1FFC */ 0x0000,
/* 1FFE */ 0x0000
/* END; */

};

void setup()
{
        Serial.begin(115200);
        clock = 0;
        P = pgm_read_word(&code[0x480]);
        IP = 0;
        S = stack;
        R = rack;
        top = 0;
        phase = 0;
```

Done Saving.

Binary sketch size: 13056 bytes (of a 32256 byte maximum)

4. Compile ceForth_328, by clicking the Compile button.

5. Upload ceForth_328 to Arduino Uno by clicking the Upload button.

6. Open HyperTerminal on PC. Set it up to 115,200 baud, 8 data bits, 1 stop bit, no parity, no flow control. ceForth_328 boots up and display this message:

```
Start Arduino
Arduino eForth, 2.0, 2011
```

7. Press Return key and the system displays:

```
    0   0 0 0 ok>
```

8. You can exercise the ceForth_328 system by typing this command:

```
WORDS
```

WORDS displays the names of all FORTH commands implemented in ceForth_328. After executing the command WORDS, the HyperTerminal console looks like the following:

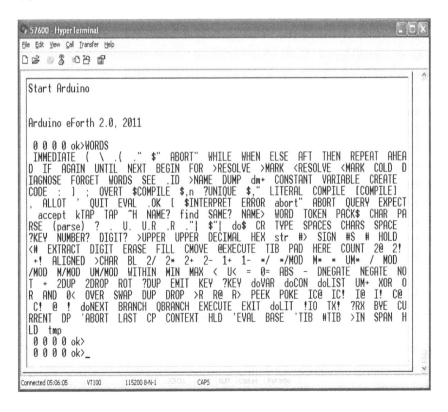

Try the following commands to verify that ceForth_328 can really compile new FORTH commands:

```
1  2  3  4
+
*
: TEST1 CR ." HELLO, WORLD!" ;
TEST1
: TEST2 IF 1 ELSE 2 THEN . ;
1 TEST2
     0   TEST2
: TEST3 10 FOR R@ . NEXT ;
TEST3
```

(Press Return key at the end of each line to send the commands to Arduino Uno.)

10. cefMETA328.f

The source code of the ceForth_328 metacompiler is contained in the file cefMETA328.f.

Here we will go through cefMETA328.f file, almost line by line to see how the ceForth_328 system is produced. All other files referred to in this file will be discussed in their separate sections.

```
( cefMEAT328.F, 13sep11cht,Arduino Uno eForth Project
) HEX
variable debugging?
\ -1 debugging? !
: .head ( addr -- addr )
    SPACE >IN @ 20 WORD COUNT TYPE >IN !
    DUP .   ;
: CR CR
    debugging? @
    IF .S KEY 0D = IF ." DONE" QUIT THEN
    THEN  ;
```

```
: BREAK CR
  .S KEY 0D = IF ." DONE" QUIT THEN    ;
: forth_' ' ;
: forth_dup DUP ;
: forth_drop DROP ;
: forth_over OVER ;
: forth_swap SWAP ;
: forth_@ @ ;
: forth_! ! ;
: forth_and AND ;
: forth_+ + ;
: forth_- - ;
: forth_word WORD ;
: forth_words WORDS ;
: forth_.s .S ;
: CRR cr ;
: forth_.( [COMPILE] .( ;
: forth_count COUNT ;
: forth_r> R> ;
: -or   XOR ;
: >body 5 + ;
: forth_forget FORGET ;
: forth_. . ;
: wf: : ;
: wf; [COMPILE] ; ; immediate
: forth_EXIT EXIT ;
: forth_QUIT quit ;
: target_' forth_' >body forth_@  ;
: -OR   XOR ;
: forth_\ [COMPILE] \ ;


CREATE ram  8000 ALLOT
: RESET   ram 8000 0 FILL ;   RESET
: RAM@    ram + W@ ;
: RAM!    ram + W! ;
: RAMC@   ram + C@ ;
: RAMC!   ram + C! ;
: FOUR    ( a -- ) 8 FOR AFT  DUP RAMC@ 5 U.R  1+
          THEN NEXT  ;
: SHOW ( a)   10 FOR AFT  CR  DUP 5 .R SPACE
      FOUR SPACE FOUR  THEN NEXT ;
: showram 0 0C FOR AFT SHOW THEN NEXT DROP ;
```

Command	Function
debugging?	A variable containing a switch to turn break points on and off. When `debugging?` is set to -1, compilation will stop and the data stack is displayed when a `cr` command is executed. Sprinkling `cr` commands in the source code file allows you to watch the progress of metacompilation and even stops it when necessary.
.head	Display name of a command that is about to be compiled. It is used to display a symbol table. You can look up the code field address of any command in this table.
cr	Pause metacompilation if `debugging?` is -1, and dump data stack.
	If you press ESC key, metacompilation is aborted. Otherwise, metacompilation continues. It just does a carriage return/line feed if `debugging?` is 0.

During metacompilation, many FORTH commands will be redefined so that they will compile tokens or assemble pseudo instructions into the target dictionary. There are numerous occasions where the original behavior of a FORTH command must be preserved. To preserve the original behavior of a FORTH command, it is assigned a different name. Thereby after a command is redefined, we can still exercise its original behavior by invoking the alternate name.

For example, + is a FORTH command that adds the top two numbers on the data stack in the F# system. Then in the cefKERN328.f file, a new + command is defined to assemble an add instruction in the target ceForth_328 system. If you still need to add two numbers, you must use the alternate command forth_+ as shown below. All the F# commands you need to use later must be redefined as forth_xxx commands. If you neglect to redefine them, you will find that the system behaves very strangely.

The ceForth_328 executes commands and accesses data in the memory range 0-1FFF. In F# we allocate a 32 KB memory array, ram, to hold the ceForth_328 target dictionary. This array contains code and data to be copied into a code array in ceForth_328, to be processed by a FORTH Virtual Machine in Arduino Uno.

ram	Memory array in F# for the ceForth_328 target dictionary. It has a logical base address of 0 in ceForth_328. Code and data words in the target are stored in this array.
ram@	Replace a logical address on stack with data fetched from ram data array.
ram!	Store second integer on stack into logical address of ram data array.
ramC@	Replace a logical address on stack with byte data fetched from ram data array.
ramC!	Store second integer on stack into logical address of ram data array as a byte.
reset	Clear ram data array, preparing it to receive code and data for ceForth_328.
four	Display 8 consecutive bytes in the target dictionary.
show	Display 256 bytes in target from address a. It also returns a +128 to show the next block of 256 bytes.
showram	Display the entire ceForth_328 dictionary of 8 KB.

```
VARIABLE hFile
: write-bin-file
   Z" mem.bin"
   $40000000 ( GENERIC_WRITE )
```

```
0 ( share mode )
0 ( security attribute )
2 ( CREATE_ALWAYS )
$80 ( FILE_ATTRIBUTE_NORMAL )
```

```
   0 ( hTemplateFile )
   CreateFileA hFile !
      hFile @
      RAM 4000
      PAD ( lpWrittenBytes )
      0 ( lpOverlapped )
      WriteFile
      IF ELSE ." write error" QUIT THEN
   hFile @ CloseHandle DROP
   ;

CREATE CRLF-ARRAY 0D C, 0A C,
: CRLF
     hFile @
     CRLF-ARRAY 2
     PAD ( lpWrittenBytes )
     0 ( lpOverlapped )
     WriteFile
     IF ELSE ." write error" QUIT THEN
  ;

: open-mif-file
   Z" rom.mif"
   $40000000 ( GENERIC_WRITE )
   0 ( share mode )
   0 ( security attribute )
   2 ( CREATE_ALWAYS )
   $80 ( FILE_ATTRIBUTE_NORMAL )
   0 ( hTemplateFile )
   CreateFileA hFile !
   ;
: write-mif-header
   CRLF
      hFile @
      $" /* WIDTH=16; */"
      PAD ( lpWrittenBytes )
      0 ( lpOverlapped )
      WriteFile
```

```
        IF ELSE ." write error" QUIT THEN
CRLF
    hFile @
    $" /* DEPTH=8192; */"
    PAD ( lpWrittenBytes )
    0 ( lpOverlapped )
    WriteFile
    IF ELSE ." write error" QUIT THEN
CRLF
    hFile @
    $" /* ADDRESS_RADIX=HEX; */"
    PAD ( lpWrittenBytes )
    0 ( lpOverlapped )
    WriteFile
    IF ELSE ." write error" QUIT THEN
CRLF
    hFile @
    $" /* DATA_RADIX=HEX; */"
    PAD ( lpWrittenBytes )
    0 ( lpOverlapped )
    WriteFile
    IF ELSE ." write error" QUIT THEN
CRLF
    hFile @
    $" /* CONTENT BEGIN; */"
    PAD ( lpWrittenBytes )
    0 ( lpOverlapped )
    WriteFile
    IF ELSE ." write error" QUIT THEN
;
```

The ceForth_328 metacompiler builds a target dictionary for the ceForth_328 in ram, a memory array in F#. This dictionary is written to a rom.mif file and will be imported to the ceForth_328 system as a code array there. The C programming language requires that the code array be written as a sequence of 16 bit integers terminated by commas. A few lines in the rom.mif file are as follows:

```
/* WIDTH=16; */
/* DEPTH=8192; */
```

```
/* ADDRESS_RADIX=HEX; */
/* DATA_RADIX=HEX; */
/* CONTENT BEGIN; */
/* 0000 */ 0x0000,
/* 0002 */ 0x0000,
/* 0004 */ 0x0000,
/* 0006 */ 0x0000,
/* 0008 */ 0x0000,
/* 08FA */ 0x0000,
/* 08FC */ 0x0000,
/* 08FE */ 0x0000,
/* 0900 */ 0x1B28,
/* 0902 */ 0x0000,
/* 0904 */ 0x0000,
/* 0906 */ 0x0000,
/* 0908 */ 0x0000,
/* 090A */ 0x0880,
/* 090C */ 0x0010,
/* 090E */ 0x1654,
/* 0910 */ 0x0000,
/* 0912 */ 0x1CE8,
/* 0914 */ 0x0320,
/* 0916 */ 0x1CE8,
/* 0918 */ 0x1702,
/* 091A */ 0x0000,
/* 091C */ 0x0000,
/* 091E */ 0x0000,
/* 0920 */ 0x0000,
 . . .
```

hFile	A variable holding a file handle.
CRLF	Insert a carriage return and a line feed into the currently opened file.
open-mif-file	Open a file named rom.mif for writing.
write-mif-line	Write one line of text into current file.
write-mif-header	Write a header required into current file.

"mif" is a term leftover from the implementation of the eP32 microprocessor on a Xilinx FPGA, and its development system expected a memory file to be in its mif format. It is easy to conform to any code format requirements by changing these xxx-mif-yyy commands here.

```
: write-mif-data
   0 ( initial ram location )
   $1000 FOR AFT
      CRLF
      hFile @
      OVER ( 4 / )   ( word address )
      <# 2F HOLD 2A HOLD 20 HOLD
         3 FOR # NEXT
      20 HOLD 2A HOLD 2F HOLD #>
      PAD ( lpWrittenBytes )
      0 ( lpOverlapped )
      WriteFile
      IF ELSE ." write error" QUIT THEN
      hFile @
      OVER RAM@
      <# 2C HOLD 3 FOR # NEXT 78 HOLD 30
                      HOLD 20 HOLD #>
      PAD ( lpWrittenBytes )
      0 ( lpOverlapped )
      WriteFile
      IF ELSE ." write error" QUIT THEN
      2+
   THEN NEXT
   DROP ( discard flash location )
   ;

: close-mif-file
   CRLF
      hFile @
      $" /* END; */"
      PAD ( lpWrittenBytes )
      0 ( lpOverlapped )
      WriteFile
      IF ELSE ." write error" QUIT THEN
   CRLF
   hFile @ CloseHandle DROP
   ;
```

```
: write-mif-file
  open-mif-file
  write-mif-header
  write-mif-data
  close-mif-file
  ;
```

write-mif-data	Write a 8 KB dictionary of the eForth System from memory array ram to the rom.mif file.
close-mif-file	Close the rom.mif file.
write-mif-file	Write a file rom.mif containing 8 KB of the eForth System according to the C code array format.

Write-mif-file opens an rom.mif file, writes a header, writes data, and then closes the file. The rom.mif file must be copied into a code array in the ceForth_328.pde file in Arduino 0022.

The ceForth_328 metacompiler continues to load the ceForth_328 assembler in cefASM328.f, the ceForth_328 kernel in cefKERN328.f, and the FORTH system in cEF328.f with the following commands:

```
FLOAD cefASM328.f
FLOAD cefKERN328.f
FLOAD cEF328.f
```

The target dictionary is complete, and can be now written out into rom.mif by the write-mif-file command.

The metacompiler now loads in the simulator in cefSIM328.f with:

```
FLOAD cefSIM328.f
```

The ceForth_328 system can now be simulated in F#. It is most satisfying to see that the output of this simulator matches exactly what is produced by the ceForth_328 system on the Arduino Uno Board. This simulator is working at pseudo instruction level. It is much more convenient to run than the Arduino 0022 system. Once a development cycle is closed in this fashion, we have very high confidence that any software change in source code of the eForth system will work on Arduino Uno, if it first passed this high-level simulator.

11. cefASM328.f

The cefASM328.f file contains a structured, optimizing assembler for ceForth_328. It packs 2 pseudo instructions into one 16-bit program word. It first clears a program location pointed to by a variable hw, and prepare it to receive 2 pseudo instructions. Assembly commands will insert pseudo instructions into consecutive bytes, and they make necessary decisions as to whether to add more instructions to the current program word, or start a new program word.

A primitive FORTH command in ceForth_328 contains a sequence of pseudo instructions, or byte codes. Two pseudo instructions are packed into a 16-bit program word. 33 pseudo instructions are defined.

The compound FORTH commands in the ceForth_328 system are based on the Token Threading Model, in which a compound command contains a list of tokens which are code field addresses of other FORTH commands. Compound commands in the form of lists of token are very compact and very efficient.

```
HEX

VARIABLE h
VARIABLE lasth 0 lasth !
            \ init linkfield address lfa
```

```
: namer! ( d -- )
  h @ ram!
        \ store double to code buffer
  1 h +!
        \ bump nameh
  ;

: COMPILE-ONLY 40 lasth @ ram@ XOR lasth @ ram! ;

: IMMEDIATE    80 lasth @ ram@ XOR lasth @
ram! ;

VARIABLE hi
VARIABLE hw
VARIABLE bi ( for byte packing)
: align   14 hi ! ;
: org   DUP . CR h !  align ;
: allot ( n -- ) h +! ;

CREATE mask  3F000000 , FC0000 ,  3F000 ,  FC0
, 3F ,

: #,    ( d ) h @ ram! 1 h +! ;
: ,w    ( d ) hw @ ram@  OR  hw @ ram! ;
: ,i    ( d ) hi @ 14 =  IF  0 hi !
h @ hw !  0 #, THEN
      hi @ mask + @ AND  ,w  4 hi +! ;
: spread ( n - d ) DUP 40 * DUP 40 * DUP 40 *
DUP
    40 * + + + + ;
: ,l    ( n ) spread ,i ;
: ,b    ( c ) bi @ 0 = IF 1 bi ! h @ hw ! 0 #,
,w
      EXIT THEN
        bi @ 1 = IF 2 bi ! 100 * ,w EXIT
THEN
        bi @ 2 = IF 3 bi ! 10000 * ,w EXIT
THEN
          0 bi ! 1000000 * ,w ;

: inst CONSTANT DOES> R> @ ,i ;
1E spread inst nop
```

```
: anew BEGIN hi @ 14 < WHILE nop REPEAT 0 bi !
;
: # ( d )  0A spread ,i  #, ;
: ldi # ;
: LIT ( d -- ) # ;
```

COMPILE-ONLY	Patch Bit 6 in first byte of name field in current target command. Text interpreter checks it to avoid executing compiler commands.
IMMEDIATE	Patch Bit 7 in first byte of name field in current target command. Compiler checks it to execute commands while compiling.

h	A variable pointing to the next free memory word at the top of the target dictionary.
lasth	A variable pointing to the name field of the current target command under construction.
namer!	Compile a 16-bit word d to the top of the target dictionary.
hw	A variable pointing to a new program word being constructed.
hi	A variable pointing to a byte to pack the next pseudo instruction.
bi	A variable pointing to a byte to pack the next ASCII character.
align	Initialize pointer hi to start assembling a new program word.
org	Initialize pointer h to a new address to start assembling.

allot	Add a n to pointer h. It skips an area in target memory and starts assembling above this area.
mask	An array of 2 masks to isolate one 8-bit pseudo instruction from a 16-bit instruction pattern. A pseudo instruction can be assembled in one of 2 bytes selected by hi.
#,	Compile d to top of target dictionary. It is the most primitive assembler and compiler. The ceForth_328 assembler is an extension of this primitive assembly command.
,w	OR d to the program word pointed to by hw. It packs a byte into the current program word.
spread	Repeat 8-bit pseudo instruction n to fill a 16-bit instruction pattern. mask uses it to select a byte code for assembling.
,i	Use hi to select one pseudo instruction in d and assemble it into the program word selected by hw.
,l	Spread an 8-bit pseudo instruction to a 16-bit pattern and assemble a pseudo instruction with ,i.
,b	Pack byte b into current program word. Pointer bi determines which byte field to pack. bi is incremented to facilitate packing of next byte.
inst	Define pseudo instruction assembly commands. It creates a pseudo instruction assembly command like a constant. When a pseudo instruction assembly command is later executed, this constant is retrieved as a byte code and a pseudo instruction is assembled into the current program word by command ,i.
nop	First pseudo instruction assembly command defined by inst.
anew	Fill current program word with a nop and initialize hi and hw to assemble new pseudo instructions in the next program word.

#	Assemble a load literal `dolit` instruction. Its literal value is assembled in the next program word pointed to by h.
lit,	Alias of #.
lit#,	Assemble a inline literal `inline` instruction. Its literal value is assembled in the next program word pointed to by h.

```
decimal \ 0 INST nop,
1   INST bye,
2   INST qrx,
3   INST txsto,
4   INST inline,
5   INST dolit,
6   INST dolist,
7   INST exit,
8   INST execu,
9   INST donext,
10  INST qbran,
11  INST bran,
12  INST store,
13  INST at,
14  INST cstor,
15  INST cat,
16  INST istore,
17  INST iat,
18  INST rfrom,
19  INST rat,
20  INST tor,
21  INST dovar,
22  INST next,
23  INST drop,
24  INST dup,
25  INST swap,
26  INST over,
27  INST duzless,
28  INST andd,
29  INST orr,
```

```
30 INST xorr,
31 INST uplus,
32 INST icat,
```

Instruction	Function
nop,	No operation.
bye,	Not used.
qrx,	Get a character from USART0 receiver
txsto	Send a character to USART0 transmitter.
inline,	Fetch next word pointer to by P and push it on stack. Increment P.
dolit	Fetch next word pointed to by IP and push it on stack. Increment IP.
dolist,	Push IP on the return stack. Copy P into IP, and execute next to start processing this new token list pointed to by the original IP.
exit,	Pop the return stack back to IP. Execute next to continue processing the token list interrupted by a compound command.
execu,	Push IP on the return stack. Pop stack into P, and start executing the pseudo instructions starting at P.
donext,	If top of return stack is not 0, decrement it and then copy the next word into IP, thus repeating a loop. If top of return stack is 0, pop it off the return stack, and increment IP, leaving this loop.
qbran,	If top of stack is 0, copy the next program word into IP, and then execute next to branch to a new token list. Otherwise, increment IP, and continue processing the current token list.
bran,	Unconditional branch to address in the next

	program word.
store,	Store the second element on stack to a location on top of stack. Pop both elements.
at,	Replace top of stack with contents of memory it addresses.
cstore,	Store the second element as a byte to a location on top of stack. Pop both elements.
cat,	Replace top of stack with contents of a byte memory it addresses.
istore,	Not used.
iat,	Not used.
rfrom,	Pop the return stack and push its top element on the stack.
rat,	Copy the top element on the return stack and push it on the stack.
tor,	Pop stack and push its top element on the return stack.
dovar,	Push the address in P on stack.
next,	Copy IP to P to process the next token. Increment IP.
drop,	Pop stack.
dup,	Duplicate top of stack.
swap,	Swap the top two elements on stack.
over,	Duplicate and push the second element on stack.
zless,	If top of stack is negative, replace it with a TRUE flag; else replace it
	with a FALSE flag.
andd,	Pop top of stack and AND it to the new top element.
orr,	Pop top of stack and OR it to the new top element.

xorr,	Pop top of stack and XOR it to the new top element.
uplus,	Add top two elements on stack, replace them with a double integer sum.
icat,	Not used.

In the ceForth_328 system, all target commands are compiled in a dictionary, and linked into a linear list. Each target command has a link field of one 16-bit word, a variable length name field in which the first byte contains a length followed by the ASCII characters of the name string, null filled to a 16-bit word boundary, and a variable-length code field containing 16-bit tokens or data words. Primitive commands have pseudo instructions in their code fields. Compound commands generally have token lists in their code fields. Following are metacompiler commands which build a header which contain a link field and a name field.

```
: begin aanew H @ ;
: ':    begin   .head CONSTANT   DOES> R> @   #, ;
hex
crr
: (makeHead)
   aanew
   20 word              \ get name of new
definition
   lastH @ nameR!       \ fill link field of last
word
   H @ lastH !          \ save nfa in lastH
   DUP c@ ,B            \ store count
     count FOR AFT
     count ,B           \ fill name field
   THEN NEXT
   DROP aanew
   ;

: makeHead
   >IN @ >R             \ save interpreter
pointer
   (makeHead)
   R> >IN !             \ restore word
```

```
pointer
    ;

: ($LIT)
    aanew 22 WORD
    count FOR AFT
        count ,B ( compile characters )
    THEN NEXT    DROP aanew ;

: $LIT ( -- )
    aanew
    22 WORD
    DUP c@ ,B ( compile count )      count FOR AFT
        count ,B ( compile characters )
    THEN NEXT    DROP aanew ;

: CODE  makeHead ': ;    \ for eForth kernel
words
```

Command	Function
begin	Mark current location in target for later address resolution.
':	Define a nameless command. begin points to the code field and is defined as a constant in the metacompiler. The run time behavior of this constant is changed to execute commands after DOES>, which uses the saved code field address to assemble a token. It also displays the name of the new command and its execution address on the terminal, with the .head command.
(makehead)	Build a header for a new target command. The header includes a link field and a name field. The address of the name field in the last target command is stored in lasth, and is compiled into the link field. h points to the name field of the new command, and is copied into lasth. Now, the following string is copied into the name

	field, starting with its length byte, and null filled to the word boundary. Now, h points to the code field of this new target command.
makehead	Build a header with (makehead) and save the name string to define a compiler command in metacompiler. It displays the name and code field address. A string can be used repeatedly by saving and restoring its pointer in a >IN word.
($LIT)	Compile a count string for a string literal.
$LIT	Compile a count string for a counted string literal.
CODE	Define a new target command. It creates a new header in the target, and then uses : to start a new subroutine. It also creates an assembly command in the metacompiler. This assembly command assembles a subroutine call instruction.

After the assembler in cefASM328.f is loaded, the metacompiler cefMETA328.f continues loading these lines of code which adds the most important compiler command : : which will be used to compile all compound commands to the target dictionary.

```
: :: makeHead begin .head CONSTANT dolist,
            aanew DOES> R> @ #, ;
: CREATE makeHead begin .head CONSTANT dovar, next,
            aanew DOES> R> @ #, ;
: VARIABLE CREATE 0 #, ;
: ;; EXIT ;
```

::	Start compiling a new compound command to the target dictionary. First build a header with the name string following. Display the name and its code field address as in a symbol table. Then, use the code field address to define a constant in the F# dictionary of the same name. When this new compound command is later referenced, a token of this code field address is added to the dictionary in the target dictionary. This is how the metacompiler builds token lists in the target dictionary.
CREATE	Build an array in target dictionary. No memory space is allocated. When referenced when the target is running, it returns its array address. Not used in ceForth_328 metacompiler.
VARIABLE	Build a variable in target dictionary. 2 bytes are allocated and initialized to 0. When referenced when the target is running, it returns the address of the variable.

With the assembler in place, we are now ready to build the ceForth_328 system in the target dictionary.

12. cefKERN328.f

In ATmega328P, there are 32 KB of flash memory, and 2 KB of RAM memory. Since the Arduino 0022 system does not allow us the write new code into the flash memory, I designed a unified memory model so that I can add new code to the RAM memory. The memory map of ceForth_328 is shown in the following table:

Address	Function
0x0 - 0xFF	ATmega328 CPU and IO registers
0x100 - 0x2FF	Data space used by C compiler

0x300 - 0x87F	Free RAM memory
0x880	Terminal input buffer
0x8FF	Start of ATmega328 hardware stack
0x900 - 0x1FFF	ceForth_328 dictionary

The parameter stack and return stack are allocated by the C compiler as parts of the FORTH Virtual Machine. We do not have to worry about them in FORTH.

We are now starting compiling new commands into the target dictionary. First, the assembly command ORG in cefMETA328.f initializes the dictionary pointer, h, to memory location $920. The memory area below $900 is mapped to the RAM memory space. The memory area from $900 to $91F stores initial values of the boot up address and system variables In the cefMETA328.f file, the following lines of commands compiles the kernel of ceForth_328.

```
$920 ORG
CR .( include kernel )
FLOAD cefKERN328.f
```

Now, cefKERN328.f is loaded to assemble primitive FORTH commands into the target dictionary, starting at $920.

System variables are variables used by the eForth system to perform all its various functions. They are defined as primitive commands, with inline, and next, pseudo instructions pointing to their respective addresses in the RAM memory, starting at location $304.

```
( cefKERN328.F, 14jan11cht, for Arduino Uno )
hex
CRR .( System variables ) CRR
CODE tmp        31E inline, next, #,
                    \ ptr to converted # string
CODE SPAN       304 inline, next, #,
                    \ #chars input by EXPECT
CODE >IN        306 inline, next, #,
                    \ input buffer offset
CODE #TIB       308 inline, next, #,
                    \ #chars in the input buffer
CODE 'TIB       30A inline, next, #,
                    \ #chars in the input buffer
CODE BASE       30C inline, next, #,
                    \ number base
CODE 'EVAL      30E inline, next, #,
                    \ interpret/compile vector
```

```
CODE HLD        310 inline, next, #,
                    \ scratch
CODE CONTEXT    312 inline, next, #,
                    \ flash vocabulary
CODE CP         314 inline, next, #,
                    \ RAM dictionary pointer
CODE LAST       316 inline, next, #,
                    \ last name in RAM vocabular
CODE 'ABORT     318 inline, next, #,
                    \ QUIT
CODE DP         31A inline, next, #,
                    \ flash dictionary pointer
CODE CURRENT    31C inline, next, #,
                    \ RAM vocabulary
```

Command	Address	Function
SPAN	304	Number of characters received by EXPECT.
>IN	306	Input buffer character pointer used by text interpreter.
#TIB	308	Length of Terminal Input Buffer.

'TIB	30A	Address of Terminal Input Buffer.
BASE	30C	Number base for numeric conversion.
'EVAL	30E	Execution vector switching between $INTERPRET and $COMPILE.
HLD	310	Pointer to a buffer holding next digit of numeric conversion.
CONTEXT	312	Dictionary pointer pointing to name field of last command in dictionary.
CP	314	Pointer to top of dictionary, the first available memory location.
LAST	316	Pointer to name field of last command in dictionary.
'ABORT	318	Execution vector to handle error condition.
tmp	31E	Pointer to a scratch pad.

Primitive commands have 2 pseudo instructions in their code fields. The assembler can pack as many pseudo instructions as needed in a code field to make the most efficient use of memory and execution time. However, in this implementation we just add a next, to a pseudo instruction to build a primitive command, which you can use interactively. If you like to enhance this system, you can use this assembler to change some compound commands into primitive commands. You can thus reduce the size of the dictionary, and also increase the execution speed.

```
CRR .( kernel words ) CRR
CODE ?RX qrx, next,
CODE TX! txsto, next,
CODE !IO nop, next,
CODE doLIT dolit, next,
CODE EXIT exit, next,
CODE EXECUTE execu, next,
CODE QBRANCH qbran, next, CODE BRANCH bran, next,
CODE doNEXT donext, next,
CODE ! store, next,
CODE @ at, next,
```

```
CODE C! cstor, next,
CODE C@ cat, next,
CODE POKE cstor, next,
CODE PEEK cat, next,
CODE R> rfrom, next,
CODE R@ rat, next,
CODE >R tor, next,
CODE DROP drop, next,
CODE DUP dup, next,
CODE SWAP swap, next,
CODE OVER over, next,
CODE 0< zless, next,
CODE AND andd, next, CODE OR orr, next,
CODE XOR xorr, next,
CODE UM+ uplus, next,
CODE doLIST dolist, next,
CODE doCON inline, next,
CODE doVAR dovar, next,
CRR
```

Primitive Command	Function
doLIT	Push next program word as a literal on the stack.
EXIT	Pop return stack into IP. Terminate a token list.
EXECUTE	Pop stack into IP to execute a token.
QBRANCH	Conditional branch to address in next program word.
BRANCH	Unconditional branch to address in next program word.
doNEXT	Loop to address in next program word.
!	Pop an address and value off stack and store value in memory.
@	Replace address on stack by its value fetched from memory.
C!	Pop an address and a byte off stack and store byte in memory.

C@	Replace address on stack by its byte value fetched from memory.
POKE	Alias of C!.
PEEK	Alias of C@.
R>	Pop return stack and push on stack.
R@	Copy top of return stack and push it on stack.
>R	Pop stack and push on return stack.
DROP	Discard top of stack.
DUP	Duplicate top of stack.
SWAP	Swap top two elements on stack.
OVER	Duplicate second element on top of stack.
0<	Replace top of stack with TRUE if it is negative. Else, replace it with FALSE.
AND	Pop stack and AND it to the new top.
OR	Pop stack and OR it to the new top.
XOR	Pop stack and XOR it to the new top.
UM+	Replace top two elements on stack with sum and carry .
doLIST	Push IP on return stack and copy P to IP. Start processing a new token list.
doCON	Push an inline literal value on stack.
doVAR	Push address in P on stack.

The kernel of ceForth_328 is completed, and the metacompiler is almost ready to compile high level commands or the compound commands. In compound commands there are lots of control structures in the token lists, and the metacompiler needs tools to construct them. We just redefine the familiar control structure commands like IF, ELSE, THEN, FOR, NEXT, BEGIN, AGAIN, UNTIL, WHILE, and REPEAT, and use them to build control structures in the target dictionary.

```
: ;; EXIT ;

: BEGIN   ( -- a )          begin ;
: AGAIN   ( a -- )          BRANCH #, ;
: UNTIL   ( a -- )          QBRANCH #, ;
: IF      ( -- a )          QBRANCH BEGIN 0 #, ;
: ELSE    ( a1 -- a2 )      BRANCH BEGIN 0 #, forth_swap
                            BEGIN forth_swap RAM! ;
: THEN    ( a -- )          BEGIN forth_swap RAM! ;
: WHILE   ( a1 -- a2 a1 )   IF forth_swap ;
: REPEAT  ( a -- )          BRANCH #, THEN ;
: AFT     ( a1 -- a3 a2 )   forth_drop BRANCH BEGIN 0 #,
                            BEGIN forth_swap ;
: FOR     ( -- a )          >R BEGIN ;
: NEXT    ( a -- )          DONEXT #, ;
: LIT     ( n -- ) [        forth_' DOLIT >body
     forth_@ LITERAL ]      #, #, ;


CRR .    ( include eforth )
FLOAD cEF328.f
```

::	Terminate compound command by appending an EXIT token to the end of token list under construction in target dictionary.
BEGIN	Start an indefinite loop.
AGAIN	Terminate an indefinite loop with a unconditional branch.
UNTIL	Terminate an indefinite loop with a conditional branch.
IF	Start a true branch.
ELSE	Start a false branch.
THEN	Terminate a branch structure.
WHILE	Start a true branch in an indefinite loop.
REPEAT	Terminate an indefinite loop with a unconditional branch.
AFT	Start a skip branch in a definite loop.

FOR	Start a definite loop.
NEXT	Terminate a definite loop.
LIT	Compile a integer literal.

We are now ready to compile all the compound command to the ceForth_328 target dictionary with the `FLOAD   cEF328.f` commands.

13. cEF328.f

The cEF328.F. file contains compound commands to be compiled into the ceForth_328 target dictionary.   These commands are defined with the `: :` command and terminated by `; ;` command. They are like the regular `:` and `;` commands in FORTH, but they compile new ceForth_328 commands into the ceForth_328 target dictionary.

The ultimate goal of these commands is to implement an interactive operating system, or a text interpreter, which accepts a line of FORTH commands from a terminal, executes these commands in sequence, and waits for another line of commands.

The text interpreter is also called the outer interpreter in FORTH. It is functionally equivalent to an operating system on a conventional computer. It accepts commands similar to English words you type, and carries out tasks specified by these commands. As an operating system, a text interpreter could be very complicated, because of all the things it has to do.   However, because FORTH employs very simple syntax rules, and has very simple internal structures, the FORTH text interpreter is much simpler than conventional operating systems.

13.1. Common Functions

This group of compound commands are commonly used in building up the FORTH text interpreter, and writing all FORTH applications. They are coded as compound commands for portability. You can re-code in assembly to increase the execute speed.

```
CRR .( Common functions ) CRR

:: ?KEY   ?RX ;;
:: KEY    BEGIN ?RX UNTIL ;;
:: EMIT   TX! ;;

:: ?DUP   ( w -- w w | 0 ) DUP IF DUP THEN ;;
:: ROT    ( w1 w2 w3 -- w2 w3 w1 ) >R SWAP R> SWAP ;;
:: 2DROP  ( w w  -- ) DROP DROP ;;
:: 2DUP   ( w1 w2 -- w1 w2 w1 w2 ) OVER OVER ;;
:: +      ( w w -- w ) UM+ DROP ;;
:: NOT    ( w -- w ) -1 LIT XOR ;;

CRR

:: NEGATE  ( n -- -n )  NOT 1 LIT + ;;
:: DNEGATE ( d -- -d )  NOT >R NOT 1 LIT UM+ R> + ;;
:: -       ( w w -- w ) NEGATE + ;;
:: ABS     ( n -- +n )  DUP 0< IF NEGATE THEN ;;

CRR .( Comparison ) CRR

:: 0=   ( w -- t )   IF 0 LIT EXIT THEN -1 LIT ;;
:: =    ( w w -- t ) XOR IF 0 LIT EXIT THEN -1 LIT ;;
:: U<   ( u u -- t ) 2DUP XOR 0< IF SWAP DROP 0< EXIT
                     THEN - 0< ;;
:: <    ( n n -- t ) 2DUP XOR 0< IF
                     DROP 0< EXIT THEN - 0< ;;
:: MAX ( n n -- n ) 2DUP       < IF SWAP THEN DROP ;;
:: MIN ( n n -- n ) 2DUP SWAP < IF SWAP THEN DROP ;;
:: WITHIN ( u ul uh -- t ) \ ul <= u < uh
  OVER - >R - R> U< ;;
```

Command	Function
?KEY	If a character is received by UASRT0 receiver, push it and TRUE on stack; else push FALSE.
KEY	Wait to receive a character and push it on stack.
EMIT	Pop stack and transmit the character.
BL	Return $20, ASCII code for space.
+!	Add second element to memory whose address is on top of stack.
?DUP	Duplicate top of stack only if it is not zero.
ROT	Rotate top 3 elements on stack
2DROP	Discard top two elements on stack.
2DUP	Duplicate top two elements on stack.
+	Pop top of stack and add it to the new top.
NOT	One's compliment top of stack.
NEGATE	Two's compliment top of stack.
DNEGATE	Two's compliment top two elements of stack as a double integer.
-	Pop top of stack and subtract it from the new top.
ABS	Replace top of stack by its absolute value.
0=	Replace top of stack with TRUE if it is zero, else with FALSE
=	Pop top two elements off stack, and push TRUE if they are equal, else push FALSE.
U<	Pop top two elements off stack, and push TRUE if second<top, else push FALSE. Comparison is unsigned.
<	Pop top two elements off stack, and push TRUE if second<top, else push FALSE. Comparison is signed.
MAX	Pop top two elements off stack, and push the larger one on top. Comparison is signed.

MIN	Pop top two elements off stack, and push the smaller one on top. Comparison is signed.
WITHIN	Pop top two elements off stack, and push TRUE if third<=top<second, else push FALSE. Comparisons are signed.

Divide and Multiply

UM/MOD and UM* are the most complicated and comprehensive division and multiplication commands. Once they are coded, all other division and multiplication operators can be derived easily from them. It has been a tradition in FORTH programming that one solves the most difficult problem first, and all other problems are solved by themselves.

The scaling commands */MOD and */ are useful in scaling number n1 by the ratio of n2/n3. When n2 and n3 are properly chosen, the scaling commands can preserve precision similar to the floating point operations at a much higher speed. Notice also that in these scaling operations, the intermediate product of n1 and n2 is a double precision integer so that the precision of scaling is maintained.

```
CRR .( Divide ) CRR

:: UM/MOD ( ud u -- ur uq )
   2DUP U<
   IF NEGATE  $0F LIT
       FOR >R DUP UM+ >R >R DUP UM+ R> + DUP
          R> R@ SWAP >R UM+   R> OR
        IF >R DROP 1 LIT + R> ELSE DROP THEN R>
       NEXT DROP SWAP EXIT
   THEN DROP 2DROP  -1 LIT DUP ;;
:: M/MOD ( d n -- r q ) \ floored
  DUP 0<  DUP >R
  IF NEGATE >R DNEGATE R>
  THEN >R DUP 0< IF R@ + THEN R> UM/MOD R>
  IF SWAP NEGATE SWAP THEN ;;
:: /MOD ( n n -- r q ) OVER 0< SWAP M/MOD ;;
```

```
:: MOD ( n n -- r ) /MOD DROP ;;
:: / ( n n -- q ) /MOD SWAP DROP ;;


CRR .( Multiply ) CRR


:: UM* ( u u -- ud )
   0 LIT SWAP ( u1 0 u2 ) $0F LIT ( 19 decimal )
   FOR DUP UM+ >R >R DUP UM+ R> + R>
     IF >R OVER UM+ R> + THEN
   NEXT ROT DROP ;;
:: * ( n n -- n ) UM* DROP ;;
:: M* ( n n -- d )
   2DUP XOR 0< >R  ABS SWAP ABS UM*  R> IF
     DNEGATE THEN ;;
:: */MOD ( n n n -- r q ) >R M* R> M/MOD ;;
:: */ ( n n n -- q ) */MOD SWAP DROP ;;
```

UM/MOD	Divide an unsigned double integer by an unsigned single integer. Return unsigned remainder and unsigned quotient.
M/MOD	Divide a signed double integer by a signed single integer. Return signed remainder and signed quotient.
/MOD	Divide a signed single integer by a signed integer. Return signed remainder and quotient.
MOD	Divide a signed single integer by a signed integer. Return signed remainder.
/	Divide a signed single integer by a signed integer. Return signed quotient.
UM*	Multiply two unsigned integers and produce an unsigned double integer product.
*	Multiply two signed integers to produce a signed single integer product.
M*	Multiply two signed integers to produce a signed double integer product.

*/MOD	Multiply signed integers n1 and n2, and then divide the double integer product by n3. Scale n1 by n2/n3. Returns both remainder and quotient.
*/	Similar to */MOD except that it only returns quotient.

Bits, Bytes and Memory

Following are commands which mostly deal with data on top of stack and in memory. A count string in FORTH is a string preceded by its length in bytes. String literals in compound commands and the name strings in the headers of command records are all count strings.

The COUNT command fetches the count byte from a count string. This address is incremented by 1, and the count just read is pushed on the stack. COUNT is designed to get the count byte at the beginning of a count string. However, it is often used in a loop to read consecutive bytes in a byte array.

```
CRR .( Bits & Bytes ) CRR

:: 1- ( a -- a ) -1 LIT + ;;
:: 1+ ( a -- a ) 1 LIT + ;;
:: 2- ( a -- a ) -2 LIT + ;;
:: 2+ ( a -- a ) 2 LIT + ;;
:: 2* ( n -- 2n ) DUP + ;;
:: 2/ ( n -- n/2 ) 2 LIT / ;;
:: BL ( -- 32 ) 20 LIT ;;
:: >CHAR ( c -- c )
   $7F LIT AND DUP $7F LIT BL WITHIN
   IF DROP ( CHAR _ ) $5F LIT THEN ;;
:: ALIGNED ( b -- a ) 1+ FFFE LIT AND ;;

CRR .( Memory access ) CRR

:: +!    ( n a -- ) SWAP OVER @ + SWAP ! ;;
:: 2!    ( d a -- ) SWAP OVER ! 2+ ! ;;
```

```
:: 2@      ( a -- d ) DUP 2+ @ SWAP @ ;;
:: COUNT ( b -- b +n ) DUP 1+ SWAP C@ ;;
:: HERE    ( -- a ) CP @ ;;
:: PAD     ( -- a ) HERE 50 LIT + ;;
:: TIB     ( -- a ) #TIB 2+ @ ;;
CRR
:: @EXECUTE ( a -- ) @ ?DUP IF EXECUTE THEN ;;
:: CMOVE      ( b b u -- )
  FOR AFT >R COUNT R@ C! R> 1+ THEN NEXT 2DROP ;;
:: FILL          ( b u c -- )
  SWAP FOR SWAP AFT 2DUP C! 1+ THEN NEXT 2DROP ;;
:: ERASE      ( b u -- ) 0 LIT FILL ;;
```

1-	Add -1 to top of stack.
1+	Add 1 to top of stack.
2-	Add -2 to top of stack
2+	Add 2 to top of stack
2*	Multiply top of stack by 2.
2/	Divide top of stack by 2.
BL	Return $20, ASCII code for space.
>CHAR	Filter non-printable character to a harmless 'underscore' character, ASCII 95.
ALIGNED	Adjust top of stack to 16-bit word boundary.
+!	Add n to a location whose address is on top of stack.
2!	Store double integer d to address on top of stack.
2@	Fetch double integer from address on top of stack.
COUNT	Push a byte fetch from address on top of stack, and increment address.
HERE	Returns address of free space above the dictionary.
PAD	Returns address of a buffer 80 bytes above the

	dictionary.
TIB	Return address of Terminal Input Buffer.
@EXECUTE	Jump to an execution address on top of stack.
CMOVE	Copy u bytes of memory from array b1 to array b2.
FILL	Fill u bytes of memory array b with the same byte c.
ERASE	Fill u bytes of memory array b with 0.

13.2. Numeric Conversion

FORTH is interesting in its special capabilities in handling numbers across a man-machine interface. It recognizes that machines and humans prefer very different representations of numbers. Machines prefer binary representation, but humans prefer decimal Arabic representation. However, depending on circumstances, a human may want numbers to be represented in other radices, like hexadecimal, octal, and sometimes binary.

FORTH solves this problem of internal (machine) versus external (human) number representations by insisting that all numbers are represented in binary form in CPU and memory. Only when numbers are imported or exported for human consumption are they converted to external ASCII representation. The radix of the external representation is stored in system variable BASE. You can select any reasonable radix in BASE, up to 72, limited by available printable characters in the ASCII character set.

Numeric Output

An output number string is built below the PAD buffer in RAM memory. The least significant digit is extracted from the integer on top of stack by dividing it by the current radix in BASE. The digit thus extracted is added to the output string backwards from PAD to the low memory. The conversion is terminated when the integer is divided to zero. The address and length of the number string are made available by #> for outputting.

An output number conversion is initiated by <# and terminated by #>. Between them, # converts one digit at a time, #S converts all the digits, while HOLD and SIGN inserts special characters into the string under construction. This set of commands is very versatile and can handle many different output formats.

```
CRR .( Numeric Output ) CRR    \ single precision

:: DIGIT    ( u -- c ) 9 LIT OVER < 7 LIT AND +
                       ( CHAR 0 ) 30 LIT + ;;
:: EXTRACT ( n base -- n c ) 0 LIT SWAP UM/MOD SWAP
DIGIT ;;
:: <#       ( -- ) PAD HLD ! ;;
:: HOLD     ( c -- ) HLD @ 1- DUP HLD ! C! ;;
:: #        ( u -- u ) BASE @ EXTRACT HOLD ;;
:: #S       ( u -- 0 ) BEGIN # DUP WHILE REPEAT ;;
CRR
:: SIGN     ( n -- ) 0< IF ( CHAR - ) 2D LIT HOLD THEN
;;
:: #>       ( w -- b u ) DROP HLD @ PAD OVER - ;;
:: str      ( n -- b u ) DUP >R ABS <# #S R> SIGN #> ;;
:: HEX      ( -- ) 10 LIT BASE ! ;;
:: DECIMAL ( -- ) 0A LIT BASE ! ;;
:: UPPER    ( c -- c' )
  DUP $61 LIT $7B LIT WITHIN IF $5F LIT AND THEN ;;
:: >UPPER   ( a -- )
  COUNT FOR AFT DUP C@ UPPER OVER C! 1+
  THEN NEXT DROP ;;
```

DIGIT	Convert integer u to a digit c.
EXTRACT	Extract least significant digit c from a number n. n is divided by radix in base.
<#	Set up HLD to start numeric conversion.
HOLD	Insert an ASCII character c in numeric output string.

#	Extract one digit from integer u, according to radix in BASE, and add it to output string.
#S	Extract all digits to output string until u is 0.
SIGN	Insert a – sign in numeric output string if n is negative.
#>	Terminate numeric conversion and return address and length of output string.
str	Convert signed integer n to a numeric output string.
HEX	Set numeric conversion radix to 16 for hexadecimal conversions.
DECIMAL	Set numeric conversion radix to 10 for decimal conversions.
UPPER	Convert a character to upper case.
>UPPER	Convert a count string pointed to by top of stack to upper case.

Numeric Input

The ceForth_328 text interpreter must interpret commands and numbers. It parses strings out of the Input Terminal Buffer and interprets them in sequence. When the text interpreter encounters a string which is not the name of a command, it assumes that the string must be a number and attempts to convert it to a number according to the current radix. When the text interpreter succeeds in converting the string to a number, the number is pushed on the parameter stack for future use, if the text interpreter is in the interpreting mode. If it is in the compiling mode, the text interpreter will compile an integer literal so that when the command under construction is later executed, the integer value will be pushed on the parameter stack.

If the text interpreter fails to convert the string to a number, this is an error condition The text interpreter aborts, post an error message to you, and then wait for your next line of commands.

```
CRR .( Numeric Input ) CRR    \ single precision

:: DIGIT?  ( c base -- u t )
  >R ( CHAR 0 ) 30 LIT - 9 LIT OVER <
  IF 7 LIT - DUP 0A LIT  < OR THEN DUP R> U< ;;
:: NUMBER? ( a -- n T | a F )
  BASE @ >R  0 LIT OVER COUNT ( a 0 b n)
  OVER C@ ( CHAR $ ) 24 LIT =
  IF HEX SWAP 1+ SWAP 1- THEN ( a 0 b' n')
  OVER C@ ( CHAR - ) 2D LIT = >R ( a 0 b n)
  SWAP R@ - SWAP R@ + ( a 0 b" n") ?DUP
  IF 1- ( a 0 b n)
     FOR DUP >R C@ BASE @ DIGIT?
        WHILE SWAP BASE @ * +  R> 1+
     NEXT DROP R@ ( b ?sign) IF NEGATE THEN SWAP
        ELSE R> R> ( b index) 2DROP ( digit number)
             2DROP 0 LIT
        THEN DUP
  THEN R> ( n ?sign) 2DROP R> BASE ! ;;
```

DIGIT?	Convert a digit c to its numeric value u according to current radix b. If conversion is successful, push a true flag above u. If not successful, return c and a false flag.
NUMBER?	Convert a count string of digits at location a to an integer. If first character is a $, convert in hexadecimal; otherwise, convert using radix in BASE. If first character is a –, negate integer. If an illegal character is encountered, address of string and a false flag are returned. Successful conversion returns integer value and a true flag.

Basic I/O

ceForth_328 system assumes that it communicates with you only through a serial I/O device. The serial I/O uses three primitive commands: ?KEY, KEY, and EMIT. These commands are enhanced to a set of compound commands which are shared by tasks doing character I/O operations.

```
CRR .( Basic I/O ) CRR

:: SPACE ( -- ) BL EMIT ;;
CRR
:: CHARS ( +n c -- ) \ ???ANS conflict
  SWAP 0 LIT MAX FOR AFT DUP EMIT THEN NEXT DROP ;;
:: SPACES ( +n -- ) BL CHARS ;;
:: TYPE ( b u -- ) FOR AFT COUNT >CHAR EMIT THEN
                   NEXT DROP ;;
:: CR ( -- ) ( =Cr ) 0D LIT EMIT ( =Lf ) 0A LIT EMIT
;;
:: do$ ( -- a )
  R> R@ R> COUNT + ALIGNED >R SWAP >R ;;
CRR
:: $"| ( -- a ) do$ ;; COMPILE-ONLY
:: ."| ( -- ) do$ COUNT TYPE ;; COMPILE-ONLY
:: .R ( n +n -- ) >R str      R> OVER - SPACES TYPE
;;
:: U.R ( u +n -- ) >R <# #S #> R> OVER - SPACES TYPE
;;
:: U. ( u -- ) <# #S #> SPACE TYPE ;;
:: . ( n -- ) BASE @ 0A LIT XOR IF U. EXIT
              THEN str SPACE TYPE ;;
:: ? ( a -- ) @ . ;;
```

SPACE	Output a blank space character.
CHARS	Output a string of n characters c.
SPACES	Output n blank space characters.
TYPE	Output n characters from a string in memory b.
CR	Output a carriage-return and a line-feed.

do$	Unpack a count string literal, pointed to by address on return stack. The string is copied to text buffer a. The return address on return stack is incremented to skip over the string literal.

String literals are data structures compiled in compound commands, in-line with other commands. A string literal must start with a string command, which knows how to handle the following count string at run time.

$"|	Unpack following count string in this string literal and return address of count string.
."|	Unpack following count string in this string literal and output string characters.
.R	Output a signed integer n right-justified in a field of +n characters.
U.R	Output an unsigned integer n right-justified in a field of +n characters.
U.	Output an unsigned integer u in free format, followed by a space.
.	Output a signed integer n in free format, followed by a space.
?	Output a signed integer stored in memory a, in free format followed by a space.

13.3. Dictionary Search

Parsing

Parsing is always considered a very advanced topic in computer science. However, because FORTH uses very simple syntax rules, parsing is easy. FORTH input stream consists of ASCII strings separated by spaces and other white space characters like tabs, carriage returns, and line feeds. The text interpreter scans the input stream, parses or separates out strings, and interprets them in sequence. After a string is parsed out of the input stream, the text interpreter interprets it; i.e., executes it if it is a valid command, compiles it if the text interpreter is in the compiling mode, and convert it to a number if the string is not a FORTH command.

```
CRR .( Parsing ) CRR

:: (parse) ( b u c -- b u delta ; <string> )
 tmp !  OVER >R  DUP \ b u u
 IF 1-  tmp C@ BL =
    IF \ b u' \ 'skip'
       FOR BL OVER C@ - 0< NOT  WHILE 1+
       NEXT ( b) R> DROP 0 LIT DUP EXIT \ all
delim
         THEN  R>
    THEN OVER SWAP \ b' b' u' \
'scan'
    FOR tmp C@ OVER C@ -  tmp C@ BL
=
       IF 0< THEN WHILE 1+
    NEXT DUP >R
       ELSE R> DROP DUP 1+ >R
       THEN OVER -  R>  R> - EXIT
  THEN ( b u) OVER R> - ;;
:: PARSE ( c -- b u ; <string> )
  >R  TIB >IN @ +  #TIB @ >IN @ -
R> (parse) >IN +! ;;
:: CHAR ( -- c ) BL PARSE DROP C@ ;;
:: PACK$ ( b u -- a )
  HERE 2+ 2DUP C!
  2DUP + 1+ 0 LIT SWAP C!
  1+ SWAP CMOVE HERE 2+ ;;
:: TOKEN ( -- a ;; <string> )
  BL PARSE 1F LIT AND PACK$ DUP >UPPER ;;
:: WORD ( c -- a ; <string> )
  PARSE PACK$ ;;
```

(parse)	Parse out a string delimited by character c from input buffer at b1, length u1. Return address b2 and length u2 of the string just parsed out, and the difference n between b1 and b2.
PARSE	Parse a string delimited by character c in TIB, from character pointed to by >IN. It returns address b and the length of parsed string u.
CHAR	Parse a string delimited by space character in TIB, and return its first character.
PACK$	Copy a string at b with length u, to a count string at a.
TOKEN	Parse out a text string delimited by a space character in TIB. The text string is assumed to be the name of a command, and its length is limited to 31 characters. This string is copied into the WORD buffer one word above the dictionary; i.e., HERE+2.
WORD	Parse out next text string delimited by character c in TIB. This string is copied into the WORD buffer one word above the dictionary; i.e., HERE+2. Length of string is limited to 255 characters.

Search Dictionary

In this FORTH system, records of commands are linked into a dictionary. A record contains three fields: a link field holding the name field address of the previous record, a name field holding the name of this command as a count string, and a code field holding the executable code of this command. The dictionary is a linear list linked through link fields and the name fields of all records.

The link field of the first command record contains a 0, indicating it is the end of the linked list. A system variable CONTEXT holds an address pointing to the name field of the last command record.

The dictionary search starts at CONTEXT and terminates at the first matched name, or at the first command record.

From CONTEXT, we locate the name field of the last command record in the dictionary. It this name does not match the string to be searched, we can find the link field of this record, which is 2 bytes less than the name field address. From the link field, we fetch out the name field of the next command record. Compare its name with the search string. And so forth.

```
CRR .( Dictionary Search ) CRR

:: NAME> ( na -- xt ) COUNT 1F LIT AND + ALIGNED ;;
:: SAME? ( b a u -- b a f \ -0+ )
  $1F LIT AND 2/
  FOR AFT OVER R@ 2* + @
          OVER R@ 2* + @ -   ?DUP
    IF R> DROP EXIT THEN THEN
  NEXT 0 LIT ;;
:: find ( a va -- xt na | a F )
                  \ *********** be careful here!!!
  SWAP            \ va a
  DUP C@ tmp !    \ va a  \ get byte count
  DUP @ >R        \ va a  \ save 1st cell
  2+ SWAP         \ a' va \ next-cell-addr va
  BEGIN DUP       \ a' na na
    IF DUP @ FF1F LIT AND  R@ XOR \ compare 1st cell
      IF 2+ -1 LIT ELSE 2+ tmp @ SAME? THEN
    ELSE R> DROP SWAP 2- SWAP EXIT \ a F
    THEN
  WHILE 2- 2- @ \ a' la
  REPEAT R> DROP SWAP DROP 2-  DUP NAME> SWAP ;;
:: NAME? ( a -- xt na | a F )
  CONTEXT @ find  ;;
```

NAME>	Return code field address xt from name field address a of a command.

SAME?	Compare two strings at a1 and a2 for u bytes. If string1>string2, returns a positive integer. If string1<string2, return a negative integer. If strings are identical, return a 0.
find	Look up a count string at a in dictionary. Search starts at va. If a command is found, return code field address xt and name field address na. If the string is not found, return address a and a false flag.
NAME?	Search dictionary from CONTEXT for a name at a. Return code field address and name field address if a command is found. Otherwise, return address a and a false flag.

13.4. Text Interpreter

Terminal Input

The text interpreter interprets source text received from an input device and stored in the Terminal Input Buffer. To process characters in the Terminal Input Buffer, we need special commands to deal with the special conditions of backspace character and carriage return. On top of stack, three special parameters are referenced in many commands: bot is the Beginning Of the input Buffer, eot is the End Of the input Buffer, and cur points to the current character in the input buffer.

```
CRR .( Terminal ) CRR

:: ^H ( bot eot cur -- bot eot cur-1 ) \ backspace
   >R OVER R> SWAP OVER XOR
   IF ( =BkSp ) 8 LIT EMIT
      1-          BL EMIT
      ( =BkSp ) 8 LIT EMIT
   THEN ;;
:: TAP ( bot eot cur c -- bot eot cur )
   DUP EMIT OVER C! 1+ ;;
```

```
:: kTAP ( bot eot cur c -- bot eot cur )
  DUP ( =Cr ) 0D LIT XOR
  IF ( =BkSp ) 8 LIT XOR IF BL TAP ELSE ^H THEN EXIT
  THEN DROP SWAP DROP DUP ;;
CRR
:: accept ( b u -- b u )
  OVER + OVER
  BEGIN 2DUP XOR
  WHILE  KEY  DUP BL -  5F LIT U<
    IF TAP ELSE kTAP THEN
  REPEAT DROP  OVER - ;;
:: EXPECT ( b u -- ) accept SPAN ! DROP ;;
:: QUERY ( -- )
  TIB 50 LIT accept #TIB !  DROP 0 LIT >IN ! ;;
```

^H	Process back-space. Erase last character and decrement cur. If cur=bot, do nothing because you cannot backup beyond beginning of input buffer.
TAP	Output character c to terminal, store c in cur, and increment cur.
	bot and eot are the beginning and end of the input buffer.
kTAP	Processes character c. c is normally stored at cur, which is incremented by 1. If c is a carriage-return, echo a space and make eot=cur. If c is a back-space, erase the last character and decrement cur.
accept	Accept u characters into buffer at b, or until a carriage return. The value of u returned is the actual count of characters received.
EXPECT	Accept u characters into buffer at b, or until a carriage return. The count of characters received is in SPAN.

QUERY	Accept up to 80 characters from the input device to the Terminal Input Buffer. This also prepares the Terminal Input Buffer for parsing by setting #TIB to characters received and clearing >IN, pointing to the beginning of the Terminal Input Buffer.

Interpreter

Text interpreter in FORTH is like a conventional operating system of a computer. It is your primary interface to get the computer to do work. Since FORTH uses very simple syntax rule--commands are separated by spaces, the text interpreter is also very simple. It accepts a line of text from the terminal, parses out a command delimited by spaces, locates the command in the dictionary and then executes it. The process is repeated until the input text is exhausted. Then the text interpreter waits for another line of text and interprets it again. This cycle repeats until you are exhausted and turns off the computer.

In ceForth_328, the text interpreter is coded as a command QUIT. QUIT contains an infinite loop which repeats the QUERY EVAL command pair. QUERY accepts a line of text from the input terminal. EVAL interprets the text one command at a time till the end of the text line.

When an error occurred, it is because the text interpreter encounters a string which can not be interpreted or processed. This string is already parsed out and stored in a buffer in RAM memory. It is displayed and followed by a ? mark, and the text interpreter is re-initialized to accept the next line of commands.

```
CRR .( Error handling ) CRR

:: ABORT ( -- ) 'ABORT
@EXECUTE ;;
:: abort" ( f -- ) IF do$
  COUNT TYPE ABORT THEN do$
DROP ;;
    COMPILE-ONLY

CRR .( Interpret ) CRR

:: ERROR ( a -- )
        space count type
$3F LIT EMIT
\          $1B LIT ( ESC)
EMIT
        ABORT
:: $INTERPRET ( a -- )
  NAME? ?DUP    IF C@ 40 LIT
AND      abort" $LIT compile
only" EXECUTE EXIT
```

```
  THEN NUMBER? IF EXIT ELSE ERROR THEN
  ;;

:: [ ( -- ) DOLIT $INTERPRET 'EVAL ! ;; IMMEDIATE
:: .OK ( -- ) DOLIT $INTERPRET 'EVAL @ =
  IF CR >R >R >R DUP . R> DUP . R> DUP . R> DUP . ."|
$LIT  ok>"
  THEN ;;
:: EVAL ( -- )
  BEGIN TOKEN DUP C@
  WHILE 'EVAL @EXECUTE \ ?STACK
  REPEAT DROP .OK ;;

CRR .( Shell ) CRR

:: QUIT ( -- )
  ( =TIB) 880 LIT 'TIB !
  [ BEGIN QUERY EVAL AGAIN ;;
```

ABORT	Execute the command whose address is in the system variable 'ABORT. This address normally points to QUIT.
abort"	When top of stack is non-zero, output the following count string and execute ABORT; otherwise, skip over the error message. It is compiled before an error message.
ERROR	Display error message in buffer at a and execute ABORT.
$INTERPRET	Processes a string at a. If it is a valid command, execute it; otherwise, convert it to a number. Failing that, execute ERROR and return to QUIT.
[	Activate interpreting mode by storing $INTERPRET into variable 'EVAL, which is executed in EVAL.
.OK	Prints the ok> prompt after dumping top 4 elements on stack.
EVAL	Interpreter loop. Parse a string from the Terminal Input Buffer. Invoke the command in 'EVAL to process it, either executing it with $INTERPRET or compiling it with $COMPILE. Repeat until input buffer is exhausted.
QUIT	Text Interpreter. Receive a line of text into Terminal Input Buffer. Process input text with EVAL. Repeat forever.

13.5. Compiler

Compiler Primitives

In the Arduino 0022 system, we cannot add new code to the flash memory. The compiler in ceForth_328 thus extends the dictionary in the RAM memory. To compile a new command, it first builds a header with a link field and a name field. Then it uses the command ' , ' (comma) to add pseudo instructions or tokens to the code field.

The compiler shares many of its functions, like parsing and dictionary search, with the text interpreter. In the end, the compiler is actually embedded in the text interpreter.

By merely changing the code field address stored in the system variable 'EVAL from $INTERPRET to $COMPILE, the text interpreter becomes a compiler. ceForth_328 switches smoothly between interpreting mode and compiling mode, and becomes a very powerful programming and debugging environment, or an operating system.

```
CRR .( Compiler Primitives ) CRR

:: ' ( -- xt ) TOKEN NAME? IF EXIT THEN ERROR
:: ALLOT ( n -- ) CP +! ;;
:: , ( w -- ) CP @ ! 2 LIT CP +! ;;
:: [COMPILE] ( -- ; <string> ) ' , ;; IMMEDIATE
CRR
:: COMPILE ( -- ) R> DUP @ , 2+ >R ;;
:: LITERAL doLIT doLIT , , ;; IMMEDIATE
:: $," ( -- ) ( CHAR " ) -2 LIT ALLOT 22 LIT
WORD
   COUNT + ALIGNED CP ! ;;

CRR .( Name Compiler ) CRR

:: ?UNIQUE ( a -- a )   DUP NAME?
   ?DUP IF COUNT 1F LIT AND SPACE TYPE ."| $LIT
reDef "
   THEN DROP ;;
:: $,n ( a -- )
   DUP @
   IF ?UNIQUE
     ( a) DUP NAME> CP !
     ( a) DUP LAST ! \ for OVERT      ( a) 2-
     ( la) CONTEXT @ SWAP ! EXIT
   THEN ERROR

CRR .( FORTH Compiler ) CRR

:: $COMPILE ( a -- )
   NAME? ?DUP
   IF C@ 80 LIT AND
     IF EXECUTE ELSE , THEN EXIT   THEN NUMBER?
   IF LITERAL EXIT
   THEN ERROR
:: OVERT ( -- ) LAST @ CONTEXT ! ;;
:: ; ( -- )
   DOLIT EXIT , [ OVERT ;; COMPILE-ONLY IMMEDIATE
:: ] ( -- ) DOLIT $COMPILE 'EVAL ! ;;
:: : ( -- ; <string> ) TOKEN $,n ( ' doLIST ) 6
LIT , ] ;;
```

'	Search dictionary for following name, and return its code field address if a command is found; otherwise, print the string with ?.
ALLOT	Allocate n bytes of memory on top of dictionary.
,	Compile an integer w to dictionary, and add it to the growing token list of the command under construction. The primitive compiler.
[COMPILE]	Compile the code field address of the next command. It compiles an immediate command, even if it would otherwise be executed.
COMPILE	Compile the code field address of the next command. It forces compilation of a command at run time.
LITERAL	Compile an integer literal. It first compiles doLIT, followed by an integer on top of stack. When doLIT is executed, it extracts the integer in the next program word and pushes it on the stack.
$,"	Compile a count string. String text is taken from the input stream and terminated by a double quote. A token (such as . " | or $ " |) must be compiled before the string to form a string literal.
?UNIQUE	Displays a warning message to show that the name of a new command is the same as a command already in the dictionary.
$,n	Build a new header in the dictionary using the name string already in the WORD buffer. Fill in the link field with the address in LAST. The top of the dictionary is now the code field of a new command, ready to accept new tokens.
$COMPILE	Process a string at a, and compile a new token in the dictionary. Increment dictionary pointer CP.

	Ready to compile next token.
OVERT	Link a new command to the dictionary and make it available for dictionary search. Change CONTEXT to point to the name field of this new command, and extend the dictionary chain to include a new command.
;	Terminate a compound command. Compile an EXIT command to terminate a token list. Link this command to the dictionary, and change the text interpreter to interpreting mode.
]	Activate compiling mode by writing the address of $COMPILE into variable 'EVAL.
:	Create a new compound command. Take the next input string to build a new header. Now, its code field is on top of the dictionary, and is ready to accept tokens.

Defining Commands

Defining commands are molds to create many commands that share the same run time execution behavior.

```
CRR .( Defining Words ) CRR

:: CODE      ( -- ; <string> )    TOKEN $,n OVERT ;;
:: CREATE    ( -- ; <string> )    CODE 1615 LIT , ;;
:: VARIABLE  ( -- ; <string> )    CREATE 0 LIT , ;;
:: CONSTANT  ( n -- ; <string> )  CODE 1604 LIT , , ;;
```

CODE	Create a new primitive command that is intended to contain pseudo instructions.
CREATE	Create a new data array without allocating memory.

| VARIABLE | Create a new variable, initialized to 0. |
| CONSTANT | Create an integer constant. |

13.6.   Tools

Memory Dump

The **DUMP** command displays 256 bytes of data starting at a memory address on top of stack. It dumps 16 bytes to a line. A line begins with the address of the first byte, followed by 16 bytes shown in hex, 3 columns per bytes. At the end of a line are the 16 bytes shown in ASCII characters. Non-printable characters are replaced by underscores (ASCII 95).

DUMP dumps RAM memory as well as flash memory. RAM memory is from 0 to $8FF, and flash memory, which is actually a data array declared in ceForth_328.pde, is from $900 to $1FFF.

The dictionary contains all command records defined in the system, ready for execution and compilation. The WORDS command allows you to examine the dictionary and to look for the correct names of commands in case you are not sure of their spellings. WORDS follows the dictionary link in the system variable CONTEXT and displays the names of all commands in the dictionary. The dictionary links can be traced easily because the link field in the header of a command points to the name field of the previous command, and the link field is two bytes below the corresponding name field.

```
CRR .( Tools ) CRR

:: dm+ ( b u -- b+u )
  OVER 5 LIT U.R SPACE FOR AFT COUNT 3 LIT U.R
THEN NEXT ;;
:: DUMP ( b -- )
  $10 LIT
  FOR AFT CR $10 LIT 2DUP dm+ ROT ROT
     SPACE TYPE
  THEN NEXT  DROP  ;;


CRR
:: >NAME ( xt -- na | F )
  CONTEXT
  BEGIN @ DUP
  WHILE 2DUP NAME> XOR
    IF 2-
    ELSE SWAP DROP EXIT
    THEN
  REPEAT SWAP DROP ;;
:: .ID ( a -- )
  ?DUP IF COUNT $1F LIT AND TYPE SPACE
  ELSE SPACE ."| $LIT {noName}" THEN ;;
:: SEE ( -- ; <string> )
  ' CR
  BEGIN
    20 LIT FOR
      2+ DUP @ DUP IF >NAME THEN ?DUP
      IF SPACE .ID ELSE DUP @ U. THEN
    NEXT KEY 0D LIT =                 \ can't
use ESC on terminal
  UNTIL DROP ;;
:: WORDS ( -- )
  CR  CONTEXT
  BEGIN @ ?DUP
  WHILE DUP SPACE .ID 2-
  REPEAT ;;
:: FORGET ( -- )
  TOKEN NAME? ?DUP   IF 2- DUP CP !
    @ DUP CONTEXT ! LAST !
    DROP EXIT
  THEN ERROR
```

dm+	Display 16 bytes from address b. Return new address b+16 for the next dm+.
DUMP	Display 256 bytes from address b. A line begins with an address, followed by 16 bytes in hex and 16 bytes in ASCII.
>NAME	From a code field address xt of a command, return its name field address na. If xt is not a valid code field address, return 0.
.ID	Display the name of a command, given its name field address a. It replaces non-printable characters in a name by underscores.
SEE	Search the next word in the input stream for a command, and decompile the first 32 program words in its code field. Display an error message if the next word is not a valid command. It scans the code field and looks for tokens. If it finds a valid token, display its name. If a word in the code field is not a token, just display its value.
WORDS	Display all names in the dictionary. The display order of commands is reversed from compiling order. The last defined command is displayed first.
FORGET	Search the next string in the input stream for a command. If it is a valid command, delete it and all subsequent command records from the dictionary.

13.7. Hardware Reset

When the ATmega328P microcontroller on Arduino Uno is powered up, or when it is reset, its FORTH Virtual Machine initializes its Finite State Machine to start running. The program counter P is initialized with the contents at location $900. The code field address of command COLD is placed at $900 by the metacompiler. The first thing COLD does is call a diagnostic routine, DIAGNOSE, to run a series of tests, verifying that the FORTH Virtual Machine is working properly. It is superfluous once the ceForth_328 is fully debugged. However, in implementing the ceForth_328, DIAGNOSE is extremely helpful in simulation and in verification. In about 1000 cycles, you can observe most pseudo instructions executed, and verify that they execute correctly.

```
::    DIAGNOSE       ( - )
      $65 LIT
\     EMIT
\ 'F'  prove UM+ 0<              \ carry, TRUE, FALSE
      0 LIT 0< -2 LIT 0<        \ 0 FFFF
      UM+ DROP                  \ FFFF ( -1)
      3 LIT UM+ UM+ DROP        \ 3
      $43 LIT UM+ DROP          \ 'F'
\     EMIT
\ 'o' logic: XOR AND OR
      $4F LIT $6F LIT XOR       \ 20h
      $F0 LIT AND
      $4F LIT OR
\     EMIT
\ 'r' stack: DUP OVER SWAP DROP
```

```
        8 LIT 6 LIT SWAP
        OVER XOR 3 LIT AND AND
        $70 LIT UM+ DROP        \ 'r'
\     EMIT
\ 't'-- prove BRANCH ?BRANCH
        0 LIT IF $3F LIT THEN
        -1 LIT IF $74 LIT ELSE $21 LIT THEN
\     EMIT
\ 'h' -- @ ! test memeory address        $68 LIT
$80 LIT !
        $80 LIT @
\     EMIT
\ 'M' -- prove >R R> R@
        $4D LIT >R R@ R> AND
\     EMIT
\ 'l'  -- prove 'next' can run
        61 LIT $A LIT FOR 1 LIT UM+ DROP NEXT
\     EMIT
\ 'emi' -- prove mul, dupy, popy
        $656D LIT $100 LIT UM*
        SWAP $100 LIT UM*
        SWAP DROP
\     EMIT EMIT
\ ' C' -- prove div
        $2043 LIT 0 LIT $100 LIT UM/MOD
\     EMIT EMIT
        ;;
```

DIAGNOSE	Test the following primitive commands in the ceForth_328: LIT, 0<, QBRANCH, UM+, DROP, XOR, AND, OR, DUP, OVER, SWAP, BRANCH, @, !, >R, R@, R>, NEXT, UM*, and UM/MOD.

COLD	Initialize the ceForth_328 system to start FORTH text interpreter. It first executes DIAGNOSE to run a few tests on most of the primitive commands, displays a sign-on message, and then jumps to QUIT. COLD is the first compound command executed after power up or after chip reset. Its address is placed in memory location $900, which contains an address the FORTH Virtual Machine uses to start its Finite State Machine.

13.8. Structures

Control Structures

Commands which build control structures in a token list are IMMEDIATE commands which are executed in compiling mode, not compiled as tokens. Control structures are as follows:

```
IF...ELSE...THEN
IF...THEN
FOR...NEXT
FOR...AFT...THEN...NEXT
BEGIN...UNTIL
BEGIN...AGAIN
BEGIN...WHILE...REPEAT
```

I use two characters a and A to denote some addresses on the data stack. a points to a location to where a branch commands would jump to. A points to a location where a new address will be stored when the address is resolved.

```
CRR .( Structures ) CRR

:: <MARK ( -- a ) HERE ;;
:: <RESOLVE ( a -- ) , ;;
:: >MARK ( -- A ) HERE 0 LIT , ;;
:: >RESOLVE ( A -- ) <MARK SWAP ! ;;
CRR
:: FOR ( -- a ) COMPILE >R <MARK ;; IMMEDIATE
:: BEGIN ( -- a ) <MARK ;; IMMEDIATE
:: NEXT ( a -- ) COMPILE doNEXT <RESOLVE ;;
IMMEDIATE :: UNTIL ( a -- ) COMPILE QBRANCH
<RESOLVE ;; IMMEDIATE
CRR
:: AGAIN ( a -- ) COMPILE  BRANCH <RESOLVE ;;
IMMEDIATE
:: IF ( -- A )   COMPILE QBRANCH >MARK ;;
IMMEDIATE
:: AHEAD ( -- A ) COMPILE BRANCH >MARK ;;
IMMEDIATE
:: REPEAT ( A a -- ) AGAIN >RESOLVE ;; IMMEDIATE
CRR
:: THEN ( A -- ) >RESOLVE ;; IMMEDIATE
:: AFT ( a -- a A ) DROP AHEAD BEGIN SWAP ;;
IMMEDIATE
:: ELSE ( A -- A )  AHEAD SWAP THEN ;; IMMEDIATE
:: WHEN ( a A -- a A a ) IF OVER ;; IMMEDIATE
:: WHILE ( a -- A a )    IF SWAP ;; IMMEDIATE


CRR .( compilers ) CRR

:: ABORT" ( -- ; <string> ) COMPILE abort" $," ;;
IMMEDIATE
:: $" ( -- ; <string> ) COMPILE $"| $," ;;
IMMEDIATE :: ." ( -- ; <string> ) COMPILE ."| $,"
;; IMMEDIATE
CRR
:: .( ( -- ) 29 LIT PARSE TYPE ;; IMMEDIATE
:: \ ( -- ) $A LIT WORD DROP ;; IMMEDIATE
:: ( 29 LIT PARSE 2DROP ;;         IMMEDIATE
:: IMMEDIATE 80 LIT LAST @ @ OR LAST @ ! ;;
```

<MARK	Leave address a of the current program word on the stack.
<RESOLVE	Compile address a into the current program word.
>MARK	Compile a 0 into current program word. Push its address A on stack.
>RESOLVE	Store address of current program word in address A on top of stack.
FOR	Begin a FOR-NEXT loop. Compile a >R command and leave the address of the next word a on the stack.
BEGIN	Begin a indefinite loop. Leave address a of the current program word on the stack.
NEXT	Compile a doNEXT command with target address a.
THEN	Resolve branch address at A with current program word address.
UNTIL	Compile a QBRANCH command with target address a.
AGAIN	Compile a BRANCH command with target address a.
IF	Compile a QBRANCH command, and leave its address a on stack.
AHEAD	Compile a BRANCH command, and leave its address a on stack.
REPEAT	Compile a BRANCH command with target address a. Use the address of the next program word to resolve the address field of the QBRANCH command at A.
AFT	Compile a BRANCH command and leave its address as A,. Replace the address a left by FOR with the address of the next program word.

ELSE	Compile a BRANCH command. and push the address of the next program word on stack. Swap two addresses on stack. Resolve the address on top of stack with current program word address.
WHILE	Compile a QBRANCH command and leave its address A on the stack. Prior address a is swapped to the top of stack.

String Structures

A string structure in a token list begins with a string command token, followed by a count string. Commands which build string structures are also IMMEDIATE commands.

ABORT"	Compile an error message. This error message is displayed when the top of the stack is non-zero.
."	Compile a string literal, which will be displayed at run time.
$"	Compile a string literal. When it is executed, only the address of the string is left on the data stack for the following commands to access this string.
.(	Display the following string, delimited by).
\	Start a comment. Ignore all characters until end of line.
(	Start a comment. Ignore the following string, delimited by).
IMMEDIATE	Set the immediate bit in the name field of the last defined command. Such a command will be executed, not compiled, in compiling mode.

13.9. Initialize System Variables

When ceForth_328 powers up, the P register is initialized by an address fetched from location $900. At the end of cefMETA328.f file, the metacompiler stores the address of COLD in this location. The metacompiler also stored 8 16-bit words in a table from $90A to $918 to initialize 8 variables, so that the FORTH Virtual Machine can run properly. The following table shows these variables, their addresses, their initial values and their functions.

```
CRR
900 ORG
COLD

$90A ORG
$880                              #,
$10                               #,
$INTERPRET
0                                    #,
lastH forth_@                     #,
$320                              #,
lastH forth_@                     #,
```

```
 QUIT

 write-mif-file
 forth_forget H
 FLOAD cefSIM328.F
```

Variable	Address	Initial Value	Function
reset vector	$900	$1ACC	Address of COLD to start ceForth_328 system.
'TIB	$90A	$880	Address of Terminal Input Buffer.
BASE	$90C	$0A	Number base for numeric conversions.

'EVAL	$90E	$15F8	Execution vector of text interpreter, initialized to point to $INTERPRET. It may be changed to point to $COMPILE in compiling mode.
HLD	$910	$0	Pointer to numeric output string.
CONTEXT	$912	$1C7C	Pointer to name field of last command in dictionary.
CP	$914	$320	Pointer to top of dictionary, first free memory location to add new commands.
LAST	$916	$1C7C	Pointer to name field of last command in dictionary.
'ABORT	$918	$16A6	Address of QUIT command to handle error conditions.

The ceForth_328 is now completely built in the target dictionary. In cefMETA328.f file, the target dictionary is now copied into the rom.mif file by the command   write-mif-file.

14. cefSIM328.f

The metacompiler redefined most F# commands in order to build the ceForth_328 target dictionary. Before we load in the simulator, the metacompiler must be removed. The commands in cefMETA328.f

```
forth_forget H
```

removes all the metacompiler commands. F# is restored and the following commands load in ceForth_328 simulator in cefSIM328.f:

```
FLOAD cefSIM328.f
```

An accurate and fast logic simulator is extremely valuable in designing and testing a new CPU or a virtual machine. It is also very useful in software development if it is difficult to debug software in actual hardware. This ceForth_328 simulator served me well in the process of developing the ceForth_328 system.

This ceForth_328 simulator faithfully replicates the logic behavior of the ceForth_328 on a cycle-by- cycle basis. The ceForth_328 FORTH Virtual Machine (FVM) is composed of a set of registers and two stacks. A 4 phase Finite State Machine (FSM) runs the FVM to execute pseudo instructions stored in a memory array. It is very simple to simulate this behavior logically in a simulator.

The source code of this simulator is in cefSIM328.F. It is loaded at the end of cefMETA328.F, which builds the ceForth_328 system in a F# memory array `ram`. The simulator reads program words from this array and executes pseudo instructions contained in this array.

14.1. Registers and Memory

```
HEX
$1F CONSTANT LIMIT ( stack depth )
$7FFF CONSTANT RANGE ( program memory size in
words )
VARIABLE CLOCK ( slot is in the last 2 bits )
VARIABLE BREAK
CREATE REGISTER $300 ALLOT
: C+! DUP >R C@ + R> C! ;
DECIMAL
REGISTER CONSTANT P
REGISTER 4 + CONSTANT I
REGISTER 8 + CONSTANT I1
REGISTER 9 + CONSTANT I2
\ REGISTER 10 + CONSTANT I3
\ REGISTER 11 + CONSTANT I4
\ REGISTER 12 + CONSTANT I5
REGISTER 13 + CONSTANT RP
REGISTER 14 + CONSTANT SP
REGISTER 16 + CONSTANT T
```

```
REGISTER 24 + CONSTANT IP
REGISTER 32 + CONSTANT WP
REGISTER $100 + CONSTANT RSTACK0
REGISTER $200 + CONSTANT SSTACK0
HEX
: RSTACK  RP C@ LIMIT AND 2 LSHIFT RSTACK0 + ;
: SSTACK  SP C@ LIMIT AND 2 LSHIFT SSTACK0 + ;
: CYCLE 1 CLOCK +! ;
: JUMP  CLOCK @ 3 OR CLOCK ! ;
: RPUSH ( n -- , push n on return stack )
    1 RP C+! RSTACK W! ;
: RPOPP ( -- n , pop n from return stack )
    RSTACK W@ -1 RP C+! ;
: SPUSH ( n -- , push n on data stack )   1 SP C+!
    T W@ SSTACK W!
    T ! ;
: SPOPP ( -- n , pop n from data stack )
    T W@
    SSTACK W@ T W!
    -1 SP C+! ;
: continue
    P W@ RAM@ DUP I W!
    100 /MOD SWAP I1 C!
    FF AND I2 C!
    2 P +! ;
```

Command	Function
LIMIT	Limit stacks depths are 32 levels.
RANGE	Limit program size to 32kB, the size of the RAM array
CLOCK	A variable that has a 30-bit count field and a 2-bit phase field. The phase field paces FSM to fetch program words and execution pseudo instructions.
BREAK	A variable holding a breakpoint address.
REGISTER	Base address of registers and stack arrays.

CYCLE	Increment CLOCK to run FSM.
JUMP	Force a 3 into phase field in CLOCK. In next cycle, CLOCK is incremented and the phase field is cleared to 0. Then, a new program word will be fetched and its pseudo instructions will be executed.
RPUSH	Push integer d on return stack.
RPOPP	Pop return stack and leave integer on system stack.
SPUSH	Push integer d on parameter stack.
SPOPP	Pop parameter stack and leave integer on system stack.
continue	Fetch next program word and store the 2 pseudo instructions in I1 and I2, to be executed in sequence by FSM.

14.2. Pseudo Instructions

Following are pseudo instructions in the FORTH Virtual Machine simulated in this simulator. These pseudo instructions were implemented in C code, which were discussed earlier in the ceForth_328.pde sketch. They are now coded in FORTH. It is interesting to compare the same set of pseudo instructions implemented in two different programming languages.

```
: next,   IP W@ RAM@ P W!
     2 IP +! JUMP ;
: nop,    JUMP ;
: bye,    ABORT" Simulation done." ;
\ : qrx,   ?RX ?DUP IF SPUSH -1 ELSE 0 THEN SPUSH ;
: qrx,    KEY SPUSH -1 SPUSH ;
: txsto,  SPOPP TX! ;
: inline, P W@ RAM@ SPUSH 2 P +! ;
: dolit,  IP W@ RAM@ SPUSH 2 IP +! next, ;
: dolist, IP W@ RPUSH P W@ IP W! next, ;
: exit,   RPOPP IP W! next, ;
```

```
: execu,   IP W@ RPUSH SPOPP P W! JUMP ;
: donext,  RPOPP ?DUP IF 1- RPUSH IP W@ RAM@ IP W!
      ELSE 2 IP +! THEN next, ;
: qbran,   SPOPP IF 2 IP +! ELSE IP W@ RAM@ IP ! THEN
next, ;
: bran,    IP W@ RAM@ IP W! next, ;
: store,   SPOPP SPOPP SWAP RAM! ;
: at,      SPOPP RAM@ SPUSH ;
: istore,  SPOPP SPOPP SWAP RAM! ;
: iat,     SPOPP RAM@ SPUSH ;
: icat,     SPOPP RAMC@ SPUSH ;
: cstor,   SPOPP SPOPP SWAP RAMC! ;
: cat,     SPOPP RAMC@ SPUSH ;
: rpat,    9C RAM@ SPUSH ;
: rpsto,   SPOPP 9C RAM! ;
: rfrom,   RPOPP SPUSH ;
: rat,     RPOPP DUP RPUSH SPUSH ;
: tor,     SPOPP RPUSH ;
: spat,    9E RAM@ SPUSH ;
: spsto,   SPOPP 9E RAM! ; : drop,   SPOPP DROP ;
```

```
: dup,    SPOPP DUP SPUSH SPUSH ;
: swap,   SPOPP SPOPP SWAP SPUSH SPUSH ;
: over,   SPOPP SPOPP DUP SPUSH SWAP SPUSH SPUSH ;
: zless,  SPOPP $8000 AND $8000 = $FFFF AND SPUSH
;
: andd,   SPOPP
SPOPP AND SPUSH
; : orr,
SPOPP SPOPP OR
SPUSH ;
: xorr,   SPOPP SPOPP XOR SPUSH ;
: uplus,  SPOPP SPOPP + DUP $FFFF AND SPUSH
          $10000 AND IF 1 ELSE 0 THEN SPUSH ;
: dovar,  P @ SPUSH ;
```

Instruction	Function
next,	Continue processing next token pointed to by IP. Increment IP.
nop,	No operation.
qrx	Push received character on stack. Also push a

	TRUE flag.
txsto,	Send a character on top of stack to transmitter.
inline,	Push next word pointer to by P on stack. Increment P.
dolit,	Push next word pointer to by IP on stack. Increment IP.
dolist,	Push IP on the return stack. Copy P into IP and start processing a new token list.
exit,	Pop the return stack back to IP. Return to an interrupted token list.
execu,	Push IP on return stack. Pop parameter stack into P, and start executing the pseudo instructions starting at P.
donext,	If top of return stack is not 0, decrement it and then jump to address pointed to by IP, thus repeating a loop. If top of return stack is 0, pop it off the return stack, increment IP, and leave this loop.
qbran,	If top of stack is 0, branch to address pointed to by IP. If top of stack is not 0, increment IP, and continue processing the current token list.
bran,	Branch to address pointed to by IP.
store,	Store the second element on stack to an address on top of stack.
cstore,	Store the second byte element on stack to an address on top of stack.
at,	Replace top of stack by the contents it addresses.
cat,	Replace top of stack by the byte contents it addresses.
icat,	Not used.
iat,	Not used.
istore,	Not used
icstore,	Not used.

rfrom	Pop the return stack and push it on the parameter stack.
rat	Pop top of return stack and push it on the parameter stack.
tor	Pop parameter stack and push it on the return stack.
drop,	Pop the parameter stack.
dup,	Duplicate top of parameter stack.
swap,	Swap the top two elements on the parameter stack.
over,	Duplicate and push the second element on the parameter stack.
zless,	If top of stack is negative, replace it with a TRUE flag; else replace it with a FALSE flag.
andd,	Pop top of parameter stack and AND it to the new top element.
orr,	Pop top of parameter stack and OR it to the new top element.
xorr,	Pop top of parameter stack and XOR it to the new top element.
uplus,	Add top two elements on parameter stack, replace them with a double integer sum.
dovar,	Push the address in P on the parameter stack.

14.3. Finite State Machine

Following is the Finite State Machine (FSM) in the FORTH Virtual Machine (FVM) implemented in the simulator. The FSM paces the simulator through pseudo instructions stored in RAM memory, with a master clock, simulated by a CLOCK variable. The lowest two bits in CLOCK is a Phase Counter. The value in the Phase Counter indicates which phase is currently being executed. If it is Phase 0, contine command is executed. If it is Phase 1, the pseudo instruction in I1 is executed. If it is Phase 2, the pseudo instruction in I1 is executed. There is nothing to do in Phase 3, and Phase 0 follows immediately.

```
HEX
CREATE CODE-TABLE
' nop,      , ' bye,      , ' qrx,      , ' txsto, ,
' inline, , ' dolit,  , ' dolist, , ' exit,   ,
' execu,  , ' donext, , ' qbran,  , ' bran,   ,
' store,  , ' at,      , ' cstor,  , ' cat,    ,
' istore, , ' iat,     , ' rfrom,  , ' rat,    ,
' tor,    , ' dovar,  , ' next,   , ' drop,   ,
' dup,    , ' swap,   , ' over,   , ' zless, ,
' andd,   , ' orr,     , ' xorr,   , ' uplus, ,
' icat,   ,

: executecode ( code -- )
   DUP 21 > ABORT" Illegal code "
   CELLS CODE-TABLE + @ EXECUTE ;

: .stack ( add # ) FOR AFT DUP @ U. 4 -
      THEN NEXT DROP CR ;
: .sstack ." S:" T @ U.
        SSTACK SP C@ .stack ;
: .rstack ." R:" RSTACK RP C@ .stack ;
: .registers ." IP=" IP @ . ." P=" P @ . ."
I="
        I @ U.
        ." I1=" I1 C@ . ." I2=" I2 C@ .
        CR ;
: S   ." CLOCK=" CLOCK @ . .registers
        .sstack .rstack ;

: SYNC0  continue ;
: SYNC1  I1 C@ executecode ;
: SYNC2  I2 C@ executecode ;
CREATE SYNC-TABLE
' continue , ' SYNC1 , ' SYNC2 , ' JUMP ,
: sync  CLOCK @ 3 AND cells
        SYNC-TABLE + @ EXECUTE ;
```

CODE-TABLE	An array containing the execution addresses of all the pseudo instructions.
executecode	From the byte code of a pseudo instruction, pick up its execution address in CODE-TABLE and execute it.
.stack	Display the contents of a stack.
.sstack	Display the contents of data stack.
.rstack	Display the contents of return stack.
.registers	Display the contents of all the relevant registers.
S	Show all the registers and stacks at this cycle.
SYNC0	Phase 0. Fetch and decode next program word
SYNC1	Phase 1. Execute pseudo instruction in I1
SYNC2	Phase 2. Execute pseudo instruction in I2
SYNC-TABLE	An array containing 4 execution addresses to be executed in 4 phases of FSM.
sync	From the phase field of variable CLOCK, execute the command appropriate for that phase, selected from SYNC-TABLE. This is the Finite State Machine of the FORTH Virtual Machine.

14.4. User Interface

This simulator has a very simple text-based user interface. The most used commands are:

```
: C       sync CYCLE S ;
: RESET REGISTER $300 ERASE 0 CLOCK !
    $900 RAM@ P ! ( start of code table in flash
)
    ;
RESET

: G       ( addr -- )
          CR ." Press any key to stop." CR
          BREAK !
          BEGIN sync P @ BREAK @ =
                IF CYCLE C EXIT
                ELSE CYCLE
                THEN
                ?KEY
          UNTIL ;
: PUSH  ( n ) T @ SPUSH T ! ;
: POP     SPOPP ;

: D       P @ CELL- FOUR FOUR ;
: M       SHOW ;
: RUN    CR ." Press ESC to stop." CR
          BEGIN C KEY 1B = UNTIL ;

: HELP  CR ." cEF Simulator, copyright Offete
Enterprises, 2009"
          CR ." C: execute next cycle"
          CR ." S: show all registers"
          CR ." D: display next 8 words"
          CR ." addr M: display 128 words from
addr"
          CR ." addr G: run and stop at addr"
          CR ." RUN: execute, one key per cycle"
          CR ;
```

Command	Function
C	Run one clock cycle and display all registers and stacks.
reset	Clear the REGISTER array, simulating hardware

	reset.
G	Run and stop at address given on stack. This is a very
	efficient way to set breakpoints and then run till a breakpoint is triggered. It allows you to execute a large portion of the program and stop only at a specified location.
PUSH	Push a new integer into the T register and data stack.
POP	Discard contents in T and pop data stack back into T.
D	Display memory starting at address in P.
M	Dump 256 bytes in memory using show command.
RUN	Continue stepping with any key, terminated by ESC.
HELP	Display instructions to use the simulator.

C is the single stepper in simulator. It runs the FSM for one cycle, and displays all registers and stacks. This is the most useful command to debug the ceForth_328 in the early development stage. You can see all data in all registers and stacks. In the ceForth_328 system, the first command executed is COLD, which executes a diagnostic word, DIAGNOSE. DIAGNOSE runs simple tests on most pseudo instructions. By single stepping through DIAGNOSE, you can validate most pseudo instructions. If all tests in DIAGNOSE run successfully, it is very likely the ceForth_328 will run correctly.

reset clears the REGISTER array, and initializes the simulator to run from a location whose address is stored in $900.

This simulator is most effective in debugging short sequences of program words to verify that the sequences are executed correctly. After ceForth_328 pseudo instructions are verified, use the G command to execute a long stretch of program and break only at a specified location. This allows large segments of programs to be tested. If the simulator runs forever and cannot reach the break point you specified, you can stop the G command by hitting a key on the keyboard to terminate it.

When F# runs the metacompiler to compile ceForth_328, it displays names and code field addresses of all commands compiled into the target dictionary. The display is a symbol table. You can look up a command and find its code field address. The code field addresses are the best place to set your break point. To debug a command, find its code field address and enter it with the G command. The simulator will break at the beginning of this command, and you can use the C command to single step through it.

Typing lots of C commands is tedious. The RUN command lessens your typing chore.
After executing RUN, the simulator displays registers and stacks and pauses. Pressing any key will single step Slot Machine for one cycle. You can run many steps easily this way. When you want to stop RUN, press the ESC key.

To examine memory, type an address followed by the M command. It will display 256 bytes of memory starting from that address. The D command displays 8 program words starting at this address.

If you want to start debugging at a particular address, type the address followed by the P command. This address is stored in the program counter register, P, and C or RUN commands will single step words starting at this memory address.

If you want to change the data stack to run simulation with the data you want on the stack, use PUSH and POP commands. Type a number followed by PUSH, and this number is pushed onto the data stack in the simulator. You can enter as many numbers onto stack as you like in this way. If you want to discard a number off the data stack, type POP.

The above commands allow you to set up the ceForth_328 simulator exactly the way you want before running simulation.

Appendix eForth_328 Commands

-	(n1 n2 -- n3)	Subtract n2 from n1 (n1-n2=n3).
' <name>	(-- addr)	Find <name> and leave its address.
!	(n addr --)	Store n to addr.
!IO	(--)	Initialize the serial I/O devices.
#	(n -- n/base)	Convert next digit of n and add it to output string
#>	(n -- addr n1)	Terminate numeric conversion, leaving addr and count n1.
#S	(n --)	Convert all significant digits in n to output string.
#TIB	(-- addr)	Return address of variable storing number of characters received in terminal input buffer.
$" <string>	(-- addr)	Compile a string literal. Return its address at run time.
S"|	(-- addr)	Return address of following string literal at run time.
$,n	(addr --)	Build a new dictionary header using the string at addr.
$COMPILE	(addr --)	Compile string at addr to dictionary as a token or literal.
$INTERPRET	(addr --)	Interpret string a addr. Execute it of convert it to a number.
(<text>)	(--)	Ignore comment text.
(parse)	(addr n char -- addr n delta)	Scan string delimited by char. Return found string and its offset delta.
*	(n1 n2 -- n3)	Signed multiply. Leave product.
*/	(n1 n2 n3 -- n4)	Signed multiply and divide. Leave quotient of (n1*n2)/n3.
*/MOD	(n1 n2 n3 -- n4)	Signed multiply and divide. Leave remainder of (n1*n2)/n3.
,	(n --)	Add n to parameter field of the most recently defined word.
.	(n --)	Display signed number with a trailing

		blank.
`." <text>"`	(--)	Compile <text> message. At run-time display text message.
`."!`	(--)	Display following string literal as a text message.
`.( <text>)`	(--)	Display <text> received from the input stream.
`.ID`	(addr --)	Display name of a command at addr.
`.OK`	(--)	Display ok> message.
`.R`	(n n1 --)	Display n right justified in a field of n1 character width.
`/`	(n1 n2 -- quot)	Signed division. Leave quotient of n1/n2.
`/MOD`	(n1 n2 -- rem quot)	Signed division. Leave quotient and remainder of n1/n2.
`: <name>`	(--)	Begin a compound command of <name>.
`;`	(--)	Terminate a compound command.
`?`	(addr --)	Display contents in addr.
`?DUP`	(n -- n n | 0)	Duplicate top of stack if it is not a 0.
`?KEY`	(-- char T | F)	Return input character and true, or a false if no input.
`?RX`	(-- char T | F)	Return input character and true, or a false if no input.
`?UNIQUE`	(addr --)	Display a "reDef" message if addr is an existing command.
`@`	(addr -- n)	Replace addr by number fetched from addr.
`[`	(--)	Switch from compilation to interpretation.
`[COMPILE] <name>`	(--)	Compile the word <name> in the input stream as an token.
`\ <text>`	(--)	Ignore text till end of line.
`]`	(--)	Switch from interpretation to compilation.
`^H`	(bot eot cur -- bot eot cur)	Backspace. Backup the cursor by one character.

+	(n1 n2 -- n3)	Add n1 and n2.
+!	(n addr --)	Add n to number at addr.
<	(n1 n2 -- flag)	True if n1 less than n2.
<#	(--)	Start numeric output conversion.
<MARK	(-- addr)	Push current program address on stack.
<RESOLVE	(addr --)	Compile addr to dictionary.
=	(n1 n2 -- flag)	True if n1 equals n2.
>	(n1 n2 -- flag)	True if n1 greater than n2.
>CHAR	(n -- char)	Convert n to a printable character char. Non-printable character is converted to an underscore character.

>IN	(-- addr)	Return address of a variable pointing to current character being interpreted.
>MARK	(-- addr)	Compile 0 to dictionary. Push its address on stack
>NAME	(ca -- na)	Convert a code field address to a name field address.
>R	(n --)	Pop top and push it on return stack.
>RESOLVE	(addr --)	Store address of current program word in addr.
>UPPER	(addr --)	Convert a count string at addr to upper case.
0<	(n -- flag)	True if n is negative.
0=	(n -- flag)	True if n is 0.
1-	(n -- n-1)	Decrement top.
1+	(n -- n+1)	Increment top.
2-	(n -- n-2)	Decrement top by 2.
2!	(d addr --)	Store a double integer to addr.
2*	(n -- 2n)	Multiply top by 2.
2/	(n -- n/2)	Divide top by 2.
2@	(addr -- d)	Fetch a double integer from addr.
2+	(n -- n+2)	Increment top by 2
2DROP	(d --)	Pop two numbers off stack.
2DUP	(d -- d d)	Duplicate a double integer on stack.

ABORT	(--)	Clean up stack and jump to address in 'ABORT.
'ABORT	(-- addr)	Return address to handle error condition.
abort"	(flag --)	If flag is true, display following message and ABORT.
ABS	(n -- u)	Return absolute value of top.
accept	(addr n -- addr n1)	Accept n characters to buffer at addr. Replace n with actual count n1
AFT	(--)	Branch to THEN to skip a branch in FOR-NEXT loop.
AHEAD	(--)	Branch forward to address in next word.
ALIGNED	(n -- n1)	Adjust n to the word boundary.
ALLOT	(+n --)	Add +n bytes to parameter field of the most recently word.
AND	(n1 n2 -- n3)	Logical bit-wise AND.
BASE	(-- addr)	Contain radix for numeric conversion.
BEGIN	(--)	Start an indefinite loop.
BL	(-- 32)	Push 32 on stack.
BRANCH	(flag --)	Branch to address in next program word if flag is 0.
C!	(n addr --)	Store a byte to addr.
C@	(addr -- n)	Fetch a byte from addr.
CHAR <string>	(-- char)	Push first character in the following text string.
CHARS	(n char --)	Send n characters char to the output device.
CMOVE	(addr addr1 n --)	Copy n bytes starting at addr to memory starting at addr1.
CODE <name>	(--)	Start a new primitive command.
COLD	(--)	Initialize FORTH system and start text interpreter.
COMPILE <name>	(--)	Retrieve address of the following command and compile it as a token.
CONSTANT <name>	(n --)	Define a constant. At run-time, n is pushed on the stack.
CONTEXT	(-- addr)	Return address of a variable pointing to name field of last word in dictionary.

COUNT	(addr -- addr+1 n)	Replace addr with address and count of a count string.
CP	(-- addr)	Return address of a variable pointing to first free space on dictionary.
CR	(--)	Display a new line. Carriage return and line feed.
CREATE <name>	(--)	Define an array. At run-time, its address is left on the stack.
DECIMAL	(--)	Set number base to decimal.

DIAGNOSE	(--)	Exercise all primitive commands for debugging.
DIGIT	(n -- char)	Convert digit u to a character.
DNEGATE	(d -- d1)	Negate a double integer on stack.
do$	(-- addr)	Return the address of the following compiled string.
doCON	(-- n)	Return contents of next program word.
doLIST	(--)	Start processing a new nested list.
doLIT	(-- n)	Push an inline literal.
doNEXT	(--)	Terminate a single index loop.
doVAR	(-- addr)	Return address of next program word.
DROP	(n --)	Discard top of stack.
DUMP	(addr n --)	Dump n bytes of memory starting from addr.
DUP	(n1 -- n2)	Duplicate top of stack.
ELSE	(--)	Terminate <true> clause, continue after the THEN.
EMIT	(char --)	Initialize the serial I/O devices.
ERASE	(addr n --)	Clear a n byte array at addr
ERROR	(addr --)	Display error message at addr and jump to ABORT.
EVAL	(--)	Interpret input stream in terminal input buffer.
'EVAL	(-- addr)	Return address of variable containing $INTERPRET or $COMPILE.
EXECUTE	(addr --)	Execute the command at addr.
EXIT	(--)	Terminate execution of current compound command.

EXPECT	(addr n --)	Accept n characters into buffer at addr.
EXTRACT	(n base -- n/base n1)	Extract the least significant digit n1 from n. n is divided by base.
FILL	(addr n char --)	Fill an array at address with n characters char.
find	(a va -- ca na | a 0)	Search dictionary at va for a string at a. Return ca and na if succeeded, else return a and 0.
FOR	(n --)	Setup loop. Repeat loop until limit n is decremented to 0.
FORGET <name>	(--)	Delete command <name> and all words added afterwards.
HERE	(-- addr)	Address of next available dictionary location.
HLD	(-- addr)	Return address of a variable pointing to next converted digit.
HOLD	(char --)	Add character char to the number string under conversion.
IF	(flag --)	If flag is zero, branches forward to <false> or after THEN.
IMMEDIATE	(--)	Set immediate bit in name field of last command added.
KEY	(-- char)	Get an ASCII character from the keyboard. Does not echo.
kTAP	(bot eot cur char -- bot eot cur)	Process a control character, CR or backspace.
LAST	(-- char)	Get an ASCII character from the keyboard. Does not echo.
LITERAL	(n --)	Compile number n. At run-time, n is pushed on the stack.
M*	(n1 n2 -- d)	Multiply n1 and n2. Return double integer product.
M/MOD	(d n -- mod quot)	Divide double integer d by n1. Return remainder and quotient.
MAX	(n1 n2 -- n3)	n3 is the larger of n1 and n2.
MIN	(n1 n2 -- n3)	n3 is the smaller of n1 and n2.
MOD	(n1 n2 -- mod)	Signed divide. Leaver remainder of n1/n2.

NAME?	(addr -- ca na | a F)	Search dictionary for name at addr. Return code field address and name field address if a command is found, else push a false.
NAME>	(na -- ca)	Convert a name field address to a code field address.
NEGATE	(n1 -- n2)	Two's complement.
NEXT	(--)	Decrement index and repeat loop until index is less than 0
NOT	(n1 -- n2)	Bit-wise one's complement.
NUMBER?	(addr -- n T | addr F)	Convert a string at addr to an integer and push a true flag. If it is not a number, push a false flag.
OR	(n1 n2 -- n3)	Logical bit-wise OR.
OVER	(n1 n2 -- n1 n2 n1)	Make copy of second item on stack.
OVERT	(--)	Change CONTEXT to add a new command to dictionary.
PACK$	(addr n-- addr1)	Copy a string at addr with length n, to a count string at addr1.
PAD	(-- addr)	Return address of a scratch pad area.
PARSE	(char -- addr n)	Parse terminal input buffer for a string terminated by char. Return its address and length.
PEEK	(addr -- n)	Fetch a byte from addr.
POKE	(n addr --)	Store a byte to addr.
QBRANCH	(flag --)	Branch to address in next word if flag is zero.
QUERY	(-- addr)	Leave address of a scratch area of at least 84 bytes.
QUIT	(--)	Return to terminal, no stack change, no message.
R@	(-- n)	Copy top of return stack on stack.
R>	(-- n)	Pop top of return stack and push it on stack.
REPEAT	(--)	Unconditional backward branch to BEGIN.
ROT	(n1 n2 n3 -- n2 n3 n1)	Rotate third item to top. "rote"

SAME?	(addr1 addr2 n -- aadr1 addr2 flag)	Compare two strings at addr1 and addr2 for n bytes. If string1>string2, returns a positive integer. If string1<string2, return a negative integer. If strings are identical, return a 0.
SEE <name>	(--)	Decompile the word <name>.
SIGN	(n --)	If n is negative, add a - sign to the number output string.
SPACE	(--)	Display a space.
str	(n -- addr n1)	Convert signed integer n to a numeric output string at addr, length n1.
SPACES	(n --)	Display n spaces.
SWAP	(n1 n2 -- n2 n1)	Exchange top two stack items.
TAP	(bot eot cur char -- bot eot cur)	Accept and echo a character and bump the cursor.
THEN	(--)	Terminate the IF-ELSE structure.
TIB	(-- addr)	Push address of terminal input buffer.
'TIB	(-- addr)	Return address of variable pointing to terminal input buffer.
tmp	(-- addr)	Return address of a temporary variable.
TOKEN	(-- addr)	Parse next string delimited by space into a word buffer 2 bytes above the top of dictionary.
TX!	(char --)	Send character c to the output device.
TYPE	(addr +n --)	Display a string of +n characters starting at address addr.
U.	(n --)	Display unsigned number with trailing blank.
U.R	(n n1 --)	Display unsigned number n right justified in a field of n1 characters.
U<	(n1 n2 -- flag)	Unsigned compare. Return true if n1<n2.
UM*	(n1 n2 -- d)	Unsigned multiply. Return double integer product.
UM/MOD	(d n -- mod quot)	Unsigned divide. Return remainder and quotient.
UM+	(n1 n2 -- d)	Unsigned add. Return double integer sum.

UNTIL	(flag --)	Repeat <loop-body> until the flag is non-zero.
UPPER	(char -- char1)	Convert a character to upper case.
VARIABLE <name>	(--)	Define a variable. At run-time, <name> leaves its address.
WHILE	(flag --)	Repeat <loop-body> and <true> clause while the flag is non-zero.
WITHIN	(n1 n2 n3 -- flag)	Return true flag if n1<=n3<n2. Else, return false flag.
WORD <text>	(char -- addr)	Get the char delimited string <text> from the input stream and leave as a counted string at addr.
WORDS	(--)	Display all commands in the dictionary.
XOR	(n1 n2 -- n3)	Logical bit-wise exclusive OR.

Additional Chapter: 17 Lessons

(as original by C-H Ting – not tested yet   - Juergen Pintaske)

```
\   +++++++++++++++++++++++++++++++++++++++++++++++++++++++++++++++++
( Example 1.    The Universal Greeting )

DECIMAL

: HELLO CR ." Hello, world!" ;

\   +++++++++++++++++++++++++++++++++++++++++++++++++++++++++++++++++
( Example 2.    The Big F )

: bar    CR ." *****" ;
: post   CR ." *    " ;
: F      bar post bar post post post ;

( Type 'F' and a return on your keyboard, and you will see a large
F character displayed on the screen )

\   +++++++++++++++++++++++++++++++++++++++++++++++++++++++++++++++++
( Example 3.    FIG, Forth Interest Group )

: center CR ."   *   " ;
: sides  CR ." *   *" ;
: triad1 CR ." * * *" ;
: triad2 CR ." **  *" ;
: triad3 CR ." *  **" ;
: triad4 CR ."  *** " ;
: quart  CR ." ** **" ;
: right  CR ." * ***" ;
: bigT   bar center center center center center center ;
: bigI   center center center center center center center ;
: bigN   sides triad2 triad2 triad1 triad3 triad2 sides ;
: bigG   triad4 sides post right triad1 sides triad4 ;
: FIG    F bigI bigG ;


\   +++++++++++++++++++++++++++++++++++++++++++++++++++++++++++++++++


( Example 4.    Repeated Patterns )

FOR      [ index -- ]          Set up loop given the index.
NEXT     [ -- ]                Decrement index by 1.
If index<0, exit.              If index=limit, exit loop; otherwise
                               Otherwise repeat after FOR.
R@       [ -- index ]          Return the current loop index. )


VARIABLE WIDTH                 ( number of asterisks to print )
```

```
: ASTERISKS ( -- , print n asterisks on the screen, n=width )
        WIDTH @                ( limit=width, initial index=0 )
        FOR ." *"              ( print one asterisk at a time )
        NEXT                   ( repeat n times )
        ;

: RECTANGLE ( height width -- , print a rectangle of asterisks )
        WIDTH !                ( initialize width to be printed )
        FOR     CR
                ASTERISKS      ( print a line of asterisks )
        NEXT
        ;

: PARALLELOGRAM ( height width -- )
        WIDTH !
        FOR     CR R@ SPACES   ( shift the lines to the right )
                ASTERISKS      ( print one line )
        NEXT
        ;

: TRIANGLE ( width -- , print a triangle area with asterisks )
        FOR     CR
                R@ WIDTH !     ( increase width every line )
                ASTERISKS      ( print one line )
        NEXT
        ;

( Try the following instructions:

        3 10 RECTANGLE
        5 18 PARALLELOGRAM
        12 TRIANGLE   )
```

\   +++

(Example 5.   The Theory That Jack Built)
(This example shows you how to build a hiararchical structure in
Forth)

DECIMAL

```
: the            ." the " ;
: that           CR ." That " ;
: this           CR ." This is " the ;
: jack           ." Jack Builds" ;
: summary        ." Summary" ;
: flaw           ." Flaw" ;
: mummery        ." Mummery" ;
: k              ." Constant K" ;
: haze           ." Krudite Verbal Haze" ;
: phrase         ." Turn of a Plausible Phrase" ;
: bluff          ." Chaotic Confusion and Bluff" ;
: stuff          ." Cybernatics and Stuff" ;
: theory         ." Theory " jack ;
: button         ." Button to Start the Machine" ;
: child          ." Space Child with Brow Serene" ;
: cybernatics    ." Cybernatics and Stuff" ;
```

```
: hiding          CR ." Hiding " the flaw ;
: lay             that ." Lay in " the theory ;
: based           CR ." Based on " the mummery ;
: saved           that ." Saved " the summary ;
: cloak           CR ." Cloaking " k ;
: thick           IF that ELSE CR ." And " THEN
                  ." Thickened " the haze ;
: hung            that ." Hung on " the phrase ;
: cover           IF that ." Covered "
                  ELSE CR ." To Cover "
                  THEN bluff ;
: make            CR ." To Make with " the cybernatics ;
: pushed          CR ." Who Pushed " button ;
: without         CR ." Without Confusion, Exposing the Bluff" ;

: rest                                  ( pause for user interaction
)
        ." . "                          ( print a period )
        10 SPACES                       ( followed by 10 spaces )
        KEY                             ( wait the user to press a
key )
        DROP CR CR CR ;

(
KEY      [ -- char ]            Wait for a keystroke, and return the
                                ASCII code of the key pressed.
DROP     [ n -- ]              Discard the number.
SPACE    [ -- ]                Display a blank.
SPACES   [ n -- ]             Display n blanks.
IF       [ f -- ]             If the flag is 0, skip the following
                                instructions up to ELSE or THEN.  If
                                flag is not 0, execute the following
                                instructions up to ELSE and skip to
                                THEN.
ELSE     [ -- ]                Skip the following instructions
                                up to THEN.
THEN     [ -- ]                Terminate an IF-ELSE-THEN structure
                                or an IF-THEN structure.
)

: cloaked cloak saved based hiding lay rest ;

: THEORY
        CR this theory rest
        this flaw lay rest
        this mummery hiding lay rest
        this summary based hiding lay rest
        this k saved based hiding lay rest
        this haze cloaked
        this bluff hung 1 thick cloaked
        this stuff 1 cover hung 0 thick cloaked
        this button make 0 cover hung 0 thick cloaked
        this child pushed
                CR ." That Made with " cybernatics without hung
                CR ." And, Shredding " the haze cloak
                CR ." Wrecked " the summary based hiding
                CR ." And Demolished " the theory rest
        ;
```

```
( Type THEORY to start)

\   ++++++++++++++++++++++++++++++++++++++++++++++++++++++++++++++++

( Example 6.    Help )
( How to use Forth interpreter to carry on a dialog )

: question
        CR CR ." Any more problems you want to solve?"
        CR ." What kind ( sex, job, money, health ) ?"
        CR
        ;

: help  CR
        CR ." Hello!  My name is Creating Computer."
        CR ." Hi there!"
        CR ." Are you enjoying yourself here?"
        KEY 32 OR 89 =
        CR
        IF      CR ." I am glad to hear that."
        ELSE    CR ." I am sorry about that."
                CR ." maybe we can brighten your visit a bit."
        THEN
        CR ." Say!"
        CR ." I can solved all kinds of problems except those
dealing"
        CR ." with Greece. "
        question
        ;

: sex   CR CR ." Is your problem TOO MUCH or TOO LITTLE?"
        CR
        ;

: too   ;                               ( noop for syntax smoothness
)

: much  CR CR ." You call that a problem?!!  I SHOULD have that
problem."
        CR ." If it reall y bothers you, take a cold shower."
        question
        ;

: little
        CR CR ." Why are you here!"
        CR ." You should be in Tokyo or New York of Amsterdam or"
        CR ." some place with some action."
        question
        ;

: health
        CR CR ." My advise to you is:"
        CR ."      1. Take two tablets of aspirin."
        CR ."      2. Drink plenty of fluids."
        CR ."      3. Go to bed (along) ."
        question
        ;

: job   CR CR ." I can sympathize with you."
```

```
        CR ." I have to work very long every day with no pay."
        CR ." My advise to you, is to open a rental computer store."
        question
        ;

: money
        CR CR ." Sorry!  I am broke too."
        CR ." Why don't you sell encyclopedias of marry"
        CR ." someone rich or stop eating, so you won't "
        CR ." need so much money?"
        question
        ;

: HELP help ;
: H help ;
: h help ;

( Type 'help' to start )

\  ++++++++++++++++++++++++++++++++++++++++++++++++++++++++++++++
```

(Example 7. Money Exchange)

The first example we will use to demonstrate how numbers are
used in Forth is a money exchange program, which converts money
represented in different currencies. Let's start with the
following currency exchange table:

```
        33.55 NT         1 Dollar
        7.73 HK          1 Dollar
        9.47 RMB         1 Dollar
        1 Ounce Gold     285 Dollars
        1 Ounce Silver   4.95 Dollars )
```

DECIMAL

```
: NT      ( nNT -- $ )     100 3355 */  ;
: $NT     ( $ -- nNT )     3355 100 */  ;
: RMB     ( nRMB -- $ )    100 947 */  ;
: $RMB    ( $ -- nJmp )    947 100 */  ;
: HK      ( nHK -- $ )     100 773 */  ;
: $HK     ( $ -- $ )       773 100 */  ;
: GOLD    ( nOunce -- $ ) 285 *  ;
: $GOLD   ( $ -- nOunce ) 285 /  ;
: SILVER  ( nOunce -- $ ) 495 100 */  ;
: $SILVER ( $ -- nOunce ) 100 495 */  ;
: OUNCE   ( n -- n, a word to improve syntax )  ;
: DOLLARS ( n -- )        . ;
```

(With this set of money exchange words, we can do some tests:

```
        5 ounce gold .
        10 ounce silver .
        100 $NT .
        20 $RMB .
```

If you have many different currency bills in your wallet, you
can add then all up in dollars:

```
            1000 NT 500 HK + .S
            320 RMB + .S
            DOLLARS ( print out total worth in dollars )
```

```
\  ++++++++++++++++++++++++++++++++++++++++++++++++++++++++++++++++
```

(Example 8. Temperature Conversion

Converting temperature readings between Celcius and Farenheit
is also an interesting problem. The difference between temperature
conversion and money exchange is that the two temperature scales
have an offset besides the scaling factor.)

```
: F>C ( nFarenheit -- nCelcius )
        32 -
        10 18 */
        ;
```

```
: C>F ( nCelcius -- nFarenheit )
        18 10 */
        32 +
        ;
```

(Try these commands

```
90 F>C .         shows the temperature in a hot summer day and
0 C>F .          shows the temperature in a cold winter night.
```

In the above examples, we use the following Forth arithmatic
operators:

```
+        [ n1 n2 -- n1+n2 ]      Add n1 and n2 and leave sum on stack.
-        [ n1 n2 -- n1-n2 ]      Subtract n2 from n1 and leave
differrence
                                 on stack.
*        [ n1 n2 -- n1*n2 ]      Multiply n1 and n2 and leave product
                                 on stack.
/        [ n1 n2 -- n1/n2 ]      Divide n1 by n2 and leave quotient on
                                 stack.
*/       [ n1 n2 n3 -- n1*n2/n3] Multiply n1 and n2, divide the
product
                                 by n3 and leave quotient on the
stack.
.S       [ ... -- ... ]          Show the topmost 4 numbers on stack.
)
```

```
\  ++++++++++++++++++++++++++++++++++++++++++++++++++++++++++++++++
```

(Example 9. Weather Reporting.)

```
: WEATHER ( nFarenheit -- )
        DUP     55 <
        IF      ." Too cold!" DROP
        ELSE    85 <
                IF      ." About right."
                ELSE    ." Too hot!"
                THEN
        THEN
        ;
```

```
( You can type the following instructions and get some responses from
the
computer:

        90 WEATHER Too hot!
        70 WEATHER About right.
        32 WEATHER Too cold.
)
```

\   ++

```
( Example 10.  Print the multiplication table )

: ONEROW ( nRow -- )
        CR
        DUP 3 .R 3 SPACES
        1 11
        FOR     2DUP *
                4 .R
                1 +
        NEXT
        DROP ;

: MULTIPLY ( -- )
        CR CR 6 SPACES
        1 11
        FOR     DUP 4 .R 1 +
        NEXT DROP
        1 11
        FOR     DUP ONEROW 1 +
        NEXT DROP
        ;

( Type MULTIPLY to print the multiplication table )
```

\   +++

```
( Example 11.  Calendars )

( Print weekly calendars for any month in any year. )
DECIMAL

VARIABLE JULIAN                    ( 0 is 1/1/1950, good until
2050 )
VARIABLE LEAP                      ( 1 for a leap year, 0
otherwise. )
( 1461 CONSTANT 4YEARS             ( number of days in 4 years )

: YEAR ( YEAR --, compute Julian date and leap year )
        DUP
        1949 - 1461 4 */MOD        ( days since 1/1/1949 )
        365 - JULIAN !             ( 0 for 1/1/1950 )
        3 =                        ( modulus 3 for a leap year )
```

```
        IF 1 ELSE 0 THEN              ( leap year )
        LEAP !
        DUP 2000 =                    ( 2000 is not a leap year )
        IF 0 LEAP ! THEN
        2001 <                        ( correction due to 2000 )
        IF ELSE -1 JULIAN +! THEN
        ;

: FIRST ( MONTH - 1ST, 1st of a month from Jan. 1 )
        DUP 1 =
        IF DROP 0 EXIT THEN           ( 0 for Jan. 1 )
        DUP 2 =
        IF DROP 31 EXIT THEN          ( 31 for Feb. 1 )
        DUP 3 =
        IF DROP 59 LEAP @ + EXIT THEN ( 59/60 for Mar. 1 )
        4 - 30624 1000 */
        90 + LEAP @ +                 ( Apr. 1 to Dec. 1 )
        ;

: STARS 60 FOR 42 EMIT NEXT ;        ( form the boarder )

: HEADER ( -- )                      ( print title bar )
        CR STARS CR
        ."     SUN     MON     TUE    WED     THU     FRI     SAT"
        CR STARS CR                  ( print weekdays )
        ;

: BLANKS ( MONTH -- )                ( skip days not in this month
)
        FIRST JULIAN @ +             ( Julian date of 1st of month
)
        7 MOD 8 * SPACES ;           ( skip colums if not Sunday
)

: DAYS ( MONTH -- )                  ( print days in a month )
        DUP FIRST                    ( days of 1st this month )
        SWAP 1 + FIRST               ( days of 1st next month )
        OVER - 1 -                   ( loop to print the days )
        1 SWAP                       ( first day count -- )
        FOR   2DUP + 1 -
                JULIAN @ + 7 MOD     ( which day in the week? )
                IF ELSE CR THEN      ( start a new line if Sunday
)
                DUP  8 U.R           ( print day in 8 column field
)
     1999        +
        NEXT
        2DROP ;                      ( discard 1st day in this
month )

: MONTH ( N -- )                     ( print a month calendar )
        HEADER DUP BLANKS            ( print header )
        DAYS CR STARS CR ;           ( print days    )

: JANUARY      YEAR 1 MONTH ;
: FEBRUARY     YEAR 2 MONTH ;
: MARCH        YEAR 3 MONTH ;
: APRIL        YEAR 4 MONTH ;
: MAY          YEAR 5 MONTH ;
```

```
: JUNE           YEAR 6 MONTH ;
: JULY           YEAR 7 MONTH ;
: AUGUST         YEAR 8 MONTH ;
: SEPTEMBER      YEAR 9 MONTH ;
: OCTOBER        YEAR 10 MONTH ;
: NOVEMBER       YEAR 11 MONTH ;
: DECEMBER       YEAR 12 MONTH ;

( To print the calender of April 1999, type:
      1999 APRIL
)


\  +++++++++++++++++++++++++++++++++++++++++++++++++++++++++++++

( Example 12.    Sines and Cosines )
```

Sines and cosines of angles are among the most often encountered
transdential functions, useful in drawing circles and many other
different applications. They are usually computed using floating
numbers for accuracy and dynamic range. However, for graphics
applications in digital systems, single integers in the range from
-32768 to 32767 are sufficient for most purposes. We shall
study the computation of sines and cosines using the single
integers.

The value of sine or cosine of an angle lies between -1.0 and +1.0.
We choose to use the integer 10000 in decimal to represent 1.0
in the computation so that the sines and cosines can be represented
with enough precision for most applications. Pi is therefore
31416, and 90 degree angle is represented by 15708. Angles
are first reduced in to the range from -90 to +90 degrees,
and then converted to radians in the ranges from -15708 to
+15708. From the radians we compute the values of sine and
cosine.

The sines and cosines thus computed are accurate to 1 part in
10000. This algorithm was first published by John Bumgarner
in Forth Dimensions, Volume IV, No. 1, p. 7.

```
31415 CONSTANT PI
10000 CONSTANT 10K )
VARIABLE XS                           ( square of scaled angle )

: KN ( n1 n2 -- n3, n3=10000-n1*x*x/n2 where x is the angle )
        XS @ SWAP /          ( x*x/n2 )
        10000 */ NEGATE      ( -n1*x*x/n2 )
        10000 +              ( 10000-n1*x*x/n2 )
        ;

: (SIN) ( x -- sine*10K, x in radian*10K )
        DUP DUP 10000 */             ( x*x scaled by 10K )
        XS !                         ( save it in XS )
        10000 72 KN                  ( last term )
        42 KN 20 KN 6 KN             ( terms 3, 2, and 1 )
        10000 */                     ( times x )
        ;

: (COS) ( x -- cosine*10K, x in radian*10K )
        DUP 10000 */ XS !            ( compute and save x*x )
```

```
        10000 56 KN 30 KN 12 KN 2 KN        ( serial expansion )
        ;

: SIN ( degree -- sine*10K )
        31415 180 */                        ( convert to radian )
        (SIN)                               ( compute sine )
        ;

: COS ( degree -- cosine*10K )
        31415 180 */
        (COS)
        ;


( To test the routines, type:

        90 SIN .                    9999
        45 SIN .                    7070
        30 SIN .                    5000
         0 SIN .                       0
        90 COS .                       0
        45 COS .                    7071
         0 COS .                   10000 )
```

\ ++

(Example 13.   Square Root)

There are many ways to take the square root of an integer. The
special routine here was first discovered by Wil Baden. Wil
used this routine as a programming challenge while attending
a FORML Conference in Taiwan, 1984.

This algorithm is based on the fact that the square of n+1 is equal
to the sum of the square of n plus 2n+1. You start with an 0 on
the stack and add to it 1, 3, 5, 7, etc., until the sum is greater
than the integer you wished to take the root. That number when
you stopped is the square root.
)

```
: SQRT ( n -- root )
        65025 OVER U<                       ( largest square it can
handle)
        IF DROP 255 EXIT THEN               ( safety exit )
        >R                                  ( save sqaure )
        1 1                                 ( initial square and root )
        BEGIN                               ( set n1 as the limit )
                OVER R@ U<                  ( next square )
        WHILE
                DUP CELLS 1 +               ( n*n+2n+1 )
                ROT + SWAP
                1 +                         ( n+1 )
        REPEAT
        SWAP DROP
        R> DROP
        ;
```

\ ++

```
( Example 14.      Radix for Number Conversions )

DECIMAL

( : DECIMAL      10 BASE ! ; )
( : HEX          16 BASE ! ; )
: OCTAL        8 BASE !  ;
: BINARY       2 BASE !  ;

( Try converting numbers among different radices:

        DECIMAL 12345 HEX U.
        HEX ABCD DECIMAL U.
        DECIMAL 100 BINARY U.
        BINARY 101010101010 DECIMAL U.
```

Real programmers impress on novices by carrying a HP calculator
which can convert numbers between decimal and hexadecimal. A
Forth computer has this calculator built in, besides other functions.
)

```
\   +++++++++++++++++++++++++++++++++++++++++++++++++++++++++++++++


( Example 15.     ASCII Character Table )

: CHARACTER ( n -- )
        DUP EMIT HEX DUP 3 .R
        OCTAL DUP 4 .R
        DECIMAL 3 .R
        2 SPACES
        ;

: LINE  ( n -- )
        CR
        5 FOR    DUP CHARACTER
                16 +
        NEXT
        DROP ;

: TABLE  ( -- )
        32
        15 FOR  DUP LINE
                1 +
        NEXT
        DROP ;

\   +++++++++++++++++++++++++++++++++++++++++++++++++++++++++++++++

( Example 16.   Random Numbers
```

Random numbers are often used in computer simulations and computer
games. This random number generator was published in Leo Brodie's
'Starting Forth'.
)

```
VARIABLE RND                            ( seed )
HERE RND !                              ( initialize seed )
```

```
: RANDOM ( -- n, a random number within 0 to 65536 )
        RND @ 31421 *                    ( RND*31421 )
        6927 +                           ( RND*31421+6926, mod 65536)
        DUP RND !                        ( refresh he seed )
        ;

: CHOOSE ( n1 -- n2, a random number within 0 to n1 )
        RANDOM UM*                       ( n1*random to a double
product)
        SWAP DROP                        ( discard lower part )
        ;                                ( in fact divide by 65536 )

( To test the routine, type

        100 CHOOSE .
        100 CHOOSE .
        100 CHOOSE .

and varify that the results are randomly distributed betweem 0 and
99 . )

\   +++++++++++++++++++++++++++++++++++++++++++++++++++++++++++++++

( Example 17.     Guess a Number )

: GetNumber ( -- n )
        BEGIN
                CR ." Enter a Number: " ( show message )
                QUERY BL WORD NUMBER?   ( get a string )
        UNTIL                           ( repeat until a valid number
)
        ;

( With this utility instruction, we can write a game 'Guess a
Number.' )

: InitialNumber ( -- n , set up a number for the player to guess )
        CR CR CR ." What limit do you want?"
        GetNumber                        ( ask the user to enter a
number )
        CR ." I have a number between 0 and " DUP .
        CR ." Now you try to guess what it is."
        CR
        CHOOSE                           ( choose a random number )
        ;                                ( between 0 and limit )

: Check ( n1 -- , allow player to guess, exit when the guess is
correct )
        BEGIN   CR ." Please enter your guess."
                GetNumber
                2DUP =                   ( equal? )
                IF      2DROP            ( discard both numbers )
                        CR ." Correct!!!"
                        EXIT
                THEN
                OVER <
                IF      CR ." Too low."
                ELSE    CR ." Too high!"
                THEN    CR
```

```
          0 UNTIL                          ( always repeat )
          ;

: Greet ( -- )
          CR CR CR ." GUESS A NUMBER"
          CR ." This is a number guessing game.  I'll think"
          CR ." of a number between 0 and any limit you want."
          CR ." (It should be smaller than 32000.)"
          CR ." Then you have to guess what it is."
          ;

: GUESS ( -- , the game )
          Greet
          BEGIN   InitialNumber                 ( set initial number)
                  Check                         ( let player guess )
                  CR CR ." Do you want to play again? (Y/N) "
                  KEY                           ( get one key )
                  32 OR 110 =                   ( exit if it is N or
n )
          UNTIL
          CR CR ." Thank you.  Have a good day."  ( sign off )
          CR
          ;
```

(Type 'GUESS' will initialize the game and the computer will entertain
a user for a while. Note the use of the indefinite loop structure:

          BEGIN <repeat-clause> [f] UNTIL

You can jump out of the infinite loop by the instruction EXIT, which
skips all the instructions in a Forth definition up to ';', which
terminates this definition and continues to the next definition.)

Dr. Chen-Hanson Ting

Introduction:
Retired chemist-turned-engineer

For how long have you been interested in Forth: 32 years

Biography:
PhD in chemistry, University of Chicago, 1965.
Professor of chemistry in Taiwan until 1975.
Firmware engineer in Silicon Valley until retirement in 2000.
Still actively composing Forth Haikus.

Custodian of the eForth systems since 1990,
still maintaining eForth systems for Arduino,
MSP430, and various ARM microcontrollers.

Author of eP8, eP16, eP24, and eP32 microcontrollers in VHDL,
which were implemented on several FPGA chips.
Offete Enterprises, started in 1975, and is now formally closed.

However, Dr. Ting can still be contacted
through email chenhting@yahoo.com.tw

www.forth.org/whoswho.html#chting)
https://sites.google.com/offete23.com/eforth/home

Exeter 04 May 2020

www.ingramcontent.com/pod-product-compliance
Lightning Source LLC
LaVergne TN
LVHW051239050326
832903LV00028B/2469